Born on the Mountaintop began as an interactive course that the authors created and facilitated in Canada. Combining their distinct backgrounds in healthcare and business, they show how it is possible to reclaim freedom in our personal and professional lives. After receiving an overwhelmingly positive response, the authors were inspired to bring the experience to a wider audience through writing this book.

WHAT PEOPLE ARE SAYING ABOUT THE BORN ON THE MOUNTAINTOP EXPERIENCE

Born on the Mountaintop is a liberating book. The insight and awareness lead one to go beyond accepting life as it is and question what we do and why we do it. The book leads one to a deep connection within, and you feel the difference in your overall quality of life immediately.

Monica Vermani, Clinical Psychotherapist
Toronto, Canada

Born on the Mountaintop is truly an extraordinary experience. You will remember the ideas and concepts long after you read the book. It has the potential to change your self-concept if you allow it to. Just as the small seed grows into a huge tree so can these seeds of freedom grow within you. Born on the Mountaintop is well thought out and logical, spanning a wealth of intuitive knowledge. As more people take up these ideas I can't help but imagine how transformative it will be for our earth.

Marianne Karsh, M.Sc.F., Director of Arborvitae
Toronto, Canada

A journey through the labyrinth of the human mind and soul, Born on the Mountaintop helps the reader find the path towards self-acceptance and unconditional love. A truly insightful and revolutionary book that is an essential read for all who wish to know themselves.

Helen Mavromichalis, MD, PT
Montreal, Canada

In my practice I see a vast number of people with a common problem – their confidence is replaced by fear and they lack a free, internal source of self-worth. Born on the Mountaintop is a practical book with big insights. It helps people decipher their "addiction" to external sources of validation, and focus on a truer sense of self that is ultimately liberating. I have started using it as a tool in my counseling.

Tushar Mehta, MD CCFP
Brampton, Canada

Born on the Mountaintop is incredible and, yet, very credible – it pushes a button in you that you always knew you had but weren't sure how to find. You never think that just one book can change your life, that just one book can open your eyes and show you the world, show you yourself in a whole new light. But, this book does just that. This book should be a prerequisite for life.

Alexia Papadopoulos, Occupational Therapist
Montreal, Canada

Born on the Mountaintop allows the reader to become free from the societal norms that prevent them from being themselves. It allows you to get to the root of your behaviors and the underlying thoughts behind them. This awareness leads to self-discoveries that not only change you, but change those around you. In this way, a chain reaction begins almost like a domino effect. That is how powerful this book can be. Recommended for anyone, anytime - especially those in the healing professions.

Sherry Duggal, ND
North York, Canada

Born on the Mountaintop is one of the best books I have read on identifying and working through issues. Freedom and Satyam have shown us how the love we receive from others affects our ability to love and accept ourselves. We learn how this leads us to set up unachievable standards of the perfect love, for being the "good" person, and other elaborate conditions on our self-worth, leading to life-long addictive pursuits of these ideals. I recommend this transformational treasure to all my clients.

Laurie Huston, BSW, Intuitive Soul Counselor
Toronto, Canada

While reading this book, I felt in many ways that it had been created just for me. Everyone can relate to feeling a need to please and manage expectations both externally and internally. The book does not teach you how to live life in a series of steps. It leads to a heightened sense of awareness with which comes realization and an internal driving force for change. Reading Born on the Mountaintop was an intense and rewarding experience for me. It truly is a very personal and enlightening journey, and I feel that I would be less fulfilled if I had not traveled it.

Vythehi Elango, Chartered Accountant
Sydney, Australia

This book is revolutionary and inspiring. The message is powerful and important. Born on the Mountaintop helps people realize that what they are looking for is not far from where they are at.

Calvin Kang, Product Manager, Bank of Montreal
Toronto, Canada

Born on the Mountaintop was a wonderful experience for me. It helped me to identify in a gentle, uncritical manner so many of the beliefs at the root of my dissatisfaction with others, myself, and life in general. But, I think the real strength of the book lies in its focus on real techniques and strategies for escaping the cycle of cynicism and self-judgment that plagues so many of us. A new way of thinking and living without fear is possible, and Born on the Mountaintop helped me to see that. I highly recommend it.

Vickram Jain, CIBC Project Manager
Mississauga, Canada

The best thing about this book is the novel, highly logical method used to explore the motives that drive people in life. Immediately after reading this book, my approach to life — and particularly my approach to relationships with women — changed. I feel free and more open. It is hard to believe that a book can have such a pervasive impact on one's life. I continue to be surprised at how the discoveries I made while reading Born on the Mountaintop guide me in life. I think everyone can benefit from the lessons this book teaches.

Angelo Santos, Physical Therapist
Oakville, Canada

BORN *on the* MOUNTAINTOP

BORN *on the* MOUNTAINTOP

RECLAIM YOUR LIFE & UNLEASH YOUR SPIRIT

SATYAM & FREEDOM MALHOTRA

BREAKTHROUGH
PUBLISHING

Copyright © by Satyam Malhotra and Freedom Malhotra.

Printed and bound in Canada. All rights reserved. No part of this book may be reproduced or transmitted in any form or by any means, electronic or mechanical, including photocopying, recording, or by an information storage and retrieval system – except by a reviewer who may quote brief passages in a review to be printed in a magazine or newspaper – without permission in writing from the publisher.

Published by Breakthrough Publishing, P.O.Box 81053, 47B Harbour Square, Toronto, ON, M5J 2R0, Canada   First Printing 2006. Second Printing 2007.

Library and Archives Canada Cataloguing in Publication

Malhotra, Satyam
    Born on the Mountaintop: reclaim your life and unleash your spirit/ Satyam & Freedom Malhotra.

ISBN 978-0-9739329-0-4

1. Self-actualization (Psychology).   I. Malhotra, Freedom,
II. Title.
BF637.S4M346 2006
158.1   C2005-907890-1

DEDICATED TO ALL THOSE WHO
LONG TO BE FREE

ACKNOWLEDGMENTS

Too many coincidences have occurred for us to imagine that this work is our own. We are conscious of the many invisible hands and generous souls that have come to our aid and made this awakening possible. For this we are forever grateful.

We would also like to take this opportunity to thank the following people:

Our parents, Vibha and Dinesh Malhotra, for encouraging us to learn and grow from a very young age. We will never forget all that you have done for us and the many silent sacrifices you both have made.

Anita Bhandari, for your constant enthusiasm, love, and emotional support. Your complete faith and confidence in us has always been a source of strength.

Vikram Malhotra, our brother, for all your profound insights. You have dedicated countless days and nights to the editing of our book, and your many contributions have helped make Born on the Mountaintop what it is today.

Hasini Palihapitiya, Avie Cohen, and Hardev Gautam for dedicating so much time and energy into the final editing of this book. Your suggestions were invaluable. Thank you also Angelo Santos, for creating the Lucid Living sketches and your crucial help with the cover design.

We are especially grateful to all the students of the Born on the Mountaintop course that have so enthusiastically embraced and applied the concepts to their lives. Your feedback has allowed us to take Born on the Mountaintop to the next level, making it even more empowering.

Every now and then, a special person comes along who touches you in unimaginable ways. Satish Kumar, we met you at a pivotal time in our lives and are honored that you have written the Foreword to this book.

Last but not least, we would like to thank some souls that have inspired us by daring to challenge the norms and breaking free in their own way: Jiddu Krishnamurti for his uncompromising commitment to the freedom of the mind; Bruce Lee for realizing a way of living and fighting free from the tradition and conformity of classical martial arts; and Joseph Campbell for encouraging us to follow our bliss.

Contents

Foreword	i
An Introduction	1
THE STORY	7
THE MANUSCRIPT	31
The Journey Ahead	32
PART 1: AWARENESS - THE GATEWAY TO FREEDOM	37
The CLS Survey	41
The Conditional Love State	46
Conditional Love State Addictions	53
The Acceptance Of Others Addiction	62
The Perfection Addiction	66
The Appearance Addiction	71
The Success Addiction	75
"The One" Addiction	79
The Save The World Addiction	84
The Comparison Addiction	88
The Spirituality Addiction	92
The Great Expectations Addiction	96
The Conquest Addiction	100
The Productivity Addiction	103
The Criticism Addiction	107
Recalling Addictive Behaviors	111
Breaking Down Your Addictions	114

Experiencing Withdrawal	117
The Web of Slavery	119
Beliefs Are Powerful and Can Be Changed	125
The Unconditional Love State	128
Exploring the ULS	136
Weighing Your Options	144
Making the Choice	147
PART 2: MIND TRANSFORMATION - RESHAPING YOUR BELIEFS	**153**
The Awareness Journal	161
A Letter to Your CLS	164
Releasing the Past	167
Tapping into the ULS	171
Mind Scripting	174
Lucid Living	178
D-Mapping	182
PART 3: MANIFESTATION – LIBERATION THROUGH ACTION	**187**
Love of Self	190
Breaking Free by Choosing Your Actions	190
Unconditional Love Rewards Program	192
Love of Others	194
Creating Safe Spaces	195
Perceptual Shifts	196
Saying the Words	196
Sharing Your Experiences	197
Rewarding Others With Unconditional Love	198

Releasing the Past With Others	200
Making it Happen	207
PART 4: KEEPING THE COMMITMENT - STAYING THE COURSE	211
Keeping yourself Motivated	213
Removing Obstacles	214
Lifestyle Integration	216
Tracking Your Commitments	219
Self-Coaching	222
The Elusive Addiction	226
New Beginnings – A Note of Farewell	231
About the Authors	233

Foreword

It has been said to "Love your neighbor as yourself." There are two parts to this sentence. One is loving your neighbor, and the second is loving your neighbor *as you love yourself.* This second part is often ignored, but it is very important because if you do not love yourself, how can you love your neighbor? Love has to grow from within and manifest without.

But, what does loving yourself mean? Love means to accept yourself as you are and for who you are. Each and every human being is special. Each and every human being comes into this world to make a particular contribution to the universe. Accepting and realizing the uniqueness of one's self and then establishing a relationship of respect, compassion, and love with all creatures is a path to happiness. This can seem so simple. Yet, we live in a world where our freedom to experience such love has been greatly limited. From birth we have been conditioned to feel and believe many things that have made it so difficult to feel good about ourselves and respect others. Born on the Mountaintop helps us understand what has gone wrong and allows us to accept who we really are.

Sometimes we complain, "Nobody loves me" or we say, "I want to be loved." Before expressing such a complaint or desire we should ask ourselves, "Do I love myself?" If you don't love yourself and if you don't trust yourself, how can you expect someone else to love and trust you? This book reveals why most of us find ourselves incapable of such self-love and discloses how to open ourselves to experiencing a deeper love for others.

You will also uncover how much of what you take for granted is constraining you. Even your sense of identity can hamper your development. For example, you might limit yourself by saying: I am American or European. I am white or black. I am male or female. I am a socialist or capitalist. I am a Buddhist or a Christian. I am a boss or a worker. All these narrow identities can hold you back. You must break free from such narrow constructs, so that you may reach for your true and greater identity.

Each of us is a product of billions of years of evolution. Our story begins with the big bang and beyond. As an individual, you are Gaia – the earth itself, more than that, you are the universe. There is nothing out there in the universe which is not inside you. You are a microcosm of a macrocosm. You are made of earth, air, fire, water, space, time, consciousness, creativity, and imagination. These are the same elements which make up the universe. You are the sun, the moon, the stars, the earth, and the heavens. You are in all, and all is in you. You are time and timeless. Your intimate self is connected to the ultimate. By loving yourself, you can love the universe. You can finally be at ease within your body and at peace within the universe. This is the essence of the book you are holding in your hand.

When I read Born on the Mountaintop for the first time, I found it clearly practical and, yet, deeply visionary. If you, the reader, can let go of your fears, accept yourself as you are, and follow some of the suggestions made in this book, you will be able to reach the depths of your soul.

We cannot make peace with the planet unless we make peace with ourselves. This is the eternal teaching of all great religions, spiritual traditions and enlightened teachers. This book provides a way to make such peace in today's world. I congratulate the authors for writing it.

SATISH KUMAR

Editor, Resurgence magazine.
Founder of Schumacher College
Author of: *Path Without Destination,*
You are Therefore I am, & *The Buddha and the Terrorist*

An Introduction

Welcome to the Born on the Mountaintop experience. You are about to uncover an incredible breakthrough in the way you understand yourself and perceive the world. As you will soon realize, this book was not written to tell you how to live your life. We believe you should have the freedom to shape your life the way you want, and Born on the Mountaintop was developed to give you that freedom. In the pages to follow, we invite you to explore and challenge the deep-rooted beliefs that are holding you back in life. Ultimately, Born on the Mountaintop will empower you with the strength to accept who you are and the freedom to live your life the way you want.

"Man is Born Free But Everywhere He is in Chains."

These words were declared by Jean Jacques Rousseau over two hundred years ago. Still, they have as much relevance now as they did back then. However, many of the chains that bind us today are far more subtle, making them harder to detect. These chains exist inside our minds. They are the beliefs that inhibit us, and are forged by the social conditioning we have endured from the day we were born. Unless we challenge them, it will remain difficult to realize freedom from the fear, stress, and dissatisfaction in our lives. The Born on the Mountaintop journey helps you uncover the chains in your own life and reveals a revolutionary way of breaking free from them.

The Great Lie of Our Lives

In the journey to come, a very important discovery will be revealed. There is one central belief that is the root cause of most of the limitations you experience in life. This belief has been reinforced by almost all of the messages you have received from your surroundings.

Although it may be hard to understand how this is possible right now, you will soon uncover what this belief is and the tremendous impact it can have on your freedom. In fact, as long as this belief exists, it will always be difficult to find the fulfillment you seek. This belief leads to psychological addictions that, at best, give us temporary highs in life, but always leave us looking for something more.

12 Psychological Addictions

What makes the Born on the Mountaintop breakthrough especially important is that it gives you an opportunity to understand how 12 psychological addictions can dominate your experience of life. By diagnosing your own addictions, you will transform your understanding of yourself. For example, you will uncover how self-consciousness, the fear of failure, and the tendency to compare yourself with others can all come from these addictions. You will also come to realize how seemingly beneficial activities such as looking for a life-partner, seeking enlightenment, or trying to make the world a better place can become addictions that severely limit your experience of life.

A New Way

The Born on the Mountaintop journey does not end with this profound understanding of yourself. That is only the beginning! The journey gets even more insightful when you begin to explore an entirely new way of perceiving yourself that will help you break free from your psychological addictions. This will open the door to a new way of living that is no longer burdened by the fears and insecurities that have held you back. In this realm of fresh possibilities, you will have the freedom to explore what you really want and the tools to make it a reality.

A JOURNEY LIKE NO OTHER

Born on the Mountaintop is filled with insights that will help transform your life. How do we know this? We have taught the contents of this book to people from all walks of life, and many have essentially told us the same thing: it has revolutionized their life. Here are some more of the benefits you will enjoy from reading this book:

A Book Custom Made for You

Right to its core, Born on the Mountaintop is about you – your freedom to live your life on your own terms. To account for the unique needs of each person, this book was written in a special way. It includes innovative tools and exercises that form a step-by-step process of exploring your mind and heart. Each step encourages you to look inside yourself to gain your own personal insights. You will also learn practical ways to help integrate your insights into your everyday life.

Realize the Freedom to Completely Accept Yourself

We are often told to be ourselves and not worry about what people think of us. But, have you ever wondered why this is so difficult? Born on the Mountaintop will show you where the need for the acceptance of others is really coming from, and why it is so hard to be at ease with ourselves. Best of all, this book will help you to accept yourself without needing to prove anything and regardless of what people think.

Overcome your Fears, and Realize your Potential

The paralyzing grip of fear can hold you back from living life to its fullest. It drains your energy and creates unnecessary stress. As long as your fears prevail, they will remain a major obstacle to realizing your true potential. Most of us would love to be fearless, but we do not have a clear understanding of where our fears are coming from. Born on the Mountaintop reveals the root cause of your fears and helps you to uproot them at the deepest level.

Reinvent the Possibilities

By letting go of crippling beliefs, you will be freeing yourself from social forces that have been affecting you for years. Some of these forces are so subtle that it can be hard to distinguish between what you want from life and what you have been conditioned to want. This book was written to end this conflict and give you the freedom to reinvent the possibilities in your life. As you read on, you will be able to open up to your deeper motivations in life. What is it that moves you from within? What is it that your inner self longs to express, but has not been given the chance? Ultimately, the insights to come will put the decisions of how to live your life back where they belong – in your hands.

Enjoy Richer Relationships

If you are looking to deepen the relationships in your life, this book will open your heart to a love that knows no limits. This love is free from needless expectations and demands that can prevent people from understanding each other. You will also learn techniques that allow you to appreciate others for who they are.

No Shortcuts

We must warn you that Born on the Mountaintop does not teach you how to escape from your problems. No shortcuts are provided, nor any magic pills to turn your life around. This journey has been designed to help you fully confront and transform the conditioning at the heart of your dissatisfaction. If you are looking to make lasting and meaningful changes in your life, this is the book you have been waiting for.

GETTING STARTED

Let us now begin with *The Story* of Brandon Wendell, a man whose circumstances inspire him to turn his life around. The direction he chooses for himself takes him on a voyage into uncharted territories of his own being. Brandon thinks he is on an adventure to fulfill his dreams, but a fateful twist of events makes him discover something far greater.

Brandon's trip sets the stage for the journey you will be taking throughout the remainder of the book. This journey is your personal exploration into the secrets of your mind and heart. Along the way, you will uncover the insights that will help you reclaim your life and unleash your spirit.

THE STORY

1

Malaya looked at the monitor and let out a heavy sigh. She saw no hope now, and as she continued to watch Brandon lying motionless in the snow, she whispered, "Sorry I let you down my friend. I am so sorry."

Her thoughts were interrupted by the sound of a hasty knock. It had been a few minutes since she had been informed of Brandon's accident, and already she had a meeting scheduled with Doctor Nestor. Quickly wiping the tear that began to trickle down her cheek, Malaya regained her composure and buzzed him in.

Doctor Nestor was the institute's leading scientist and handled their most important projects. Knowing that Nestor had a lot of things on his mind, Malaya was not surprised to see him trip over his own feet as he entered the office. Malaya watched the all too familiar scene of Nestor picking up yet another dropped file while adjusting his eyeglasses. Getting up, Nestor nodded a quick greeting to his supervisor, Malaya, and began to examine the data on the large monitor. As he studied Brandon's situation, Malaya wasted no time.

"Nestor, it looks like this is it. We have about twenty minutes before the hypothermia sets in. More importantly, Brandon's will to survive is slipping by the second. If we do not do something quickly, all the work we have done with Brandon will be in vain. Is there anything we can do to bring him back?"

"Well," Nestor began while rubbing his chin in thought, "we are looking at a man with very little to lose. Throughout his life, Brandon has always been searching for something more. But despite everything he has tried, he has not found what he is looking for. Over these last couple of years, he has grown so dissatisfied that he has put himself in the situation he is in right now."

"Yes Nestor," Malaya interrupted impatiently, "I am well aware of all this. I have been following his case as closely as you have. I know that he has been through his share of struggles and read countless books in search of answers, yet we have still failed him. We have been unable to provide him the answers he is looking for. I cannot help but feel responsible for the situation he is in. Perhaps if we had given him better guidance, he would not be dying. Is there any hope now, Doctor?"

Although what Malaya said was not a laughing matter, Nestor could not help but smile. Her words emphasized the importance of his recent and most prized discovery. Given the open floor to speak, Nestor felt an excitement rush through his body.

"You are right Malaya. Brandon gave up on quick fixes a long time ago. That is why you have to hear me out. I have great news. We finally found a way to help people break free from the conditioning of their minds and the never-ending struggle to prove their worth. If we can only get Brandon to understand the significance of this discovery, I am confident we can help him."

Malaya had to admit that she was curious. Nestor was not the type to exaggerate his claims.

"Do you remember the CLS project from years ago?" Nestor began.

Malaya's curiosity quickly turned into annoyance. "Doctor Nestor, I strictly forbade you from putting any more of our resources into that project. It is a dead end. There is no way around it. You would have to challenge the entire system."

"Malaya, you know as much as I do, there can be no hope for real freedom of the mind and heart unless it is addressed. Besides, it is not a dead end. The team has been working on it during off-hours for years, and we finally found the way to beat it."

"You figured a way around the CLS?" she asked in disbelief.

"Yes ma'am."

"You found a way to give people the freedom to completely accept themselves without needing to acquire, achieve, or become anything? And what about all the traps? Have you found a way to avoid them?"

"Yes," Nestor replied.

"If what you say is true…this is a breakthrough. It gets to the root of the problem like never before. It can change everything. Put an end to the most destructive belief."

After some more thought, Malaya began to shake her head still struggling to digest the ramifications of Nestor's claims, "But, is he ready for this?"

"Absolutely. I ran his file through the computer earlier. He is a prime candidate. He has eight of the twelve major psychological addictions," Nestor explained.

Malaya turned to look at the monitor again, her head still shaking at the idea. While she reflected on the events that led Brandon to this point, her gaze intensified. Nestor could hardly bear the suspense of awaiting Malaya's decision any longer, until he saw the beginning of a smile appear on her face. Malaya stared into the distance as if in a daze, "I wonder," she said, "I just wonder…"

2

Thirteen Months Earlier

Alisha looked searchingly into her own eyes as she brushed her hair. She did not understand. She was finally getting close to the perfect balance she wanted in her life. Since moving in with Brandon, they had never felt so close. Both of them were satisfied with their careers and could now start on the life they hoped to spend together. But, her intuition told her something was wrong, something that she just couldn't quite put her finger on.

"Lish, what's taking so long? I thought you said we were in a rush," Brandon said as he walked in the entrance behind her. He smiled as he noticed Alisha was, once again, deep in thought. Wrapping his arms around her waist, Brandon pulled Alisha closer to him. "Hey," Brandon said while looking at her in the mirror, "where is that head of yours this time?"

Being in Brandon's arms had an immediately calming effect on her. She looked up at his reflection. "Oh nowhere," she said while letting out a sigh.

"Nowhere, huh? Well, that nowhere place of yours seems like it's very far away," he said as he smiled at her through the mirror.

"It's not that far," she said as she turned to snuggle her head into his shoulder and enjoy the embrace. Alisha was looking forward to this weekend. Remembering that they were in a rush, she pushed back against him to finish getting ready. Brandon only held her tighter, playfully resisting her as she tried to break free.

"C'mon, what's going on? Where is that mind of yours?" Brandon asked.

"Oh, it's nothing really. Just thinking about that deal of yours from work." It was a minor lie, but it was more convincing than the truth. The fact was she did not know what was bothering her.

"Oh that," Brandon said dismissively trying to push the thought out of her mind. "I told you not to worry about that. I got it all under control. It was a big loss, but I'll make up for it. Besides this is our first weekend free in ages. I don't even want to waste a moment thinking about it. Doesn't our yoga teacher say something about that? Be in the present or something. He talks about repeating that, doesn't he? Or did you miss that, cause you were too busy gawking at him again?"

Alisha laughed and gave him a playful elbow to the stomach while freeing herself. She turned around quickly and looked at him. "It's a mantra, and it's: 'Be in the now'. Looks like somebody's still a little jealous I see." She laughed teasingly. Suddenly turning serious she said, "You should be. It's not every day that a man can walk on his hands *and* share his feelings."

Brandon chuckled, "Really? It must be so refreshing."

"It is," Alisha said turning around to finish getting ready. She winked at him through the mirror. "Now c'mon, we have to go. Are the bags in the car?"

"I am putting them in now. Are you going to be ready any time soon?"

"I will be down in a second."

Although Alisha wanted to continue getting ready, she felt herself irresistibly watching Brandon's movements through the mirror. She looked at him curiously as he walked out of the bedroom door.

3

Watching the sun setting over a lake affects you in a way that few other scenes can. It is as if the blazing restlessness deep within is gradually overcome by the stillness of the water. At least that is what Brandon felt as he stood on the deck of the boat where Alisha was holding a surprise party for him. The sounds of his closest friends laughing in celebration faded into the background as he stared into the horizon.

His thoughts were interrupted by a sudden nudge on his shoulder. He turned to meet one of the few strangers at his party.

"Brandon Wendell!" the stranger said while reaching to shake Brandon's hand, "It's an honor to meet you. My name is Edwin."

Of all the people at the party, Edwin appeared the least conventional. He sported long blond hair and a face that hadn't felt a razor for at least a couple of weeks. In his excitement, Edwin shook Brandon's hand so vigorously that Brandon almost spilled his drink.

"Dude, I've been waiting to meet you in person for years," Edwin said as he swung his bangs to the side. "You have no idea what an inspiration you've been in my life."

Knowing that there was a select circle of people who still admired him, Brandon was not taken aback by Edwin's awe. "Really?" Brandon replied acting surprised.

"Don't be so modest. You were one of the youngest to climb the Nuptse summit solo. Your run of Annapurnas back then was phenomenal. And then you topped it all off with the K2 summit. You had to be one of the most promising mountain climbers of that time. I first heard about you from that magazine. What was it again? The name's on the tip of my tongue…"

"Extreme Climb," Brandon replied.

"Yeah, that's it! I probably still have a copy of it beating around somewhere. Anyway, when I heard of how young you were and how fearless, I just had to get into climbing. The rest is pretty much history. I haven't stopped climbing since. What about you? You still climb?"

It was a simple answer. He had not climbed in years. Still, Brandon felt himself swallowing hard and heard himself saying, "I do it as a hobby now. Too busy with work for the big climbs."

"Oh that's cool," Edwin said. "So what ever happened to that Everest expedition? I never heard anything about it."

Brandon's heart sank. "It never happened. I got injured." This was another lie, and though Brandon barely knew Edwin, for some reason he cared deeply about what Edwin thought of him.

"Well that's a relief. Someone told me you gave up climbing. I heard that you got over it. But I never could believe that about you. Sorry to hear about the injury. It happens to the best of 'em though. I remember I was on McKinley in Alaska, and I almost ripped my shoulder out trying to hang on. Still made it up without oxygen..." Edwin continued, but Brandon was not listening anymore. He felt faint. It was as if a wound he thought had healed long ago was now reopened.

He quickly stopped Edwin mid-sentence, "It was nice to meet you Edwin. Sorry about the ripped oxygen.... I'll see you around."

"I guess," Edwin said confused.

By now, Brandon was completely consumed in his thoughts. 'Thirty-five!' he thought. 'I am thirty-five years old now and still restless inside. Is this it? Is this the life I imagined for myself when I was peering over the mountaintops years ago?'

"Time to cut the cake." The sound of Alisha's voice helped snap him out of it. And when he looked up to see her face, his anxiety vanished. He looked around to see his friends and remembered how they admired his life. He thought about his great job, and the pride rushed back into his body. Brandon almost laughed at himself. 'What was I thinking?' he thought. 'Sometimes I forget how great my life is.' Brandon looked at the glass in his hands. He noticed his faint reflection in the drink before draining it down his throat.

"Hey Ben," he yelled to a friend at the bar. "Can you get me another?"

4

Within the walls of his cubicle, Brandon quickly scanned through his emails after lunch.

> Meet me in my office at 5 pm.
> -Mike

In a cutthroat corporate culture, an email like this from your boss is enough to make any employee nervous. But, having worked closely with Mike for years, Brandon knew the drill by now. "Damage control," he said under his breath. It was the biggest deal they had come across in five years, and Mike clumsily managed to let it slip out of their hands. Now Brandon's job was to land another deal by the end of the year.

Peering into a colleague's cubicle, he got right to business. "Maria, you got those numbers for me?" he asked, resting the weight of his folded arms on the cubicle ledge.

Maria did not respond as she sat at her desk staring aimlessly at the blank screen of her computer.

"Maria?" he said quieter.

She slowly raised her head and looked up at Brandon.

"Boo," he said managing to hide his puzzled feelings with a grin.

Forcing a smile, she responded plainly, "What's up Brandon?"

"Not much," Brandon said shrugging off his initial confusion.

"Just wanted to know if you got that file done up for us?"

"No, I'm still working on it."

"Maria, we have to get that going pronto. You know how important it is for us."

Maria seemed cold and distant. She showed no sympathy for his plight. It was during this brief moment that Brandon noticed the tears welling in her eyes and wondered if they had been there all along.

"Yes, I'm well aware of that. I'm working on it," she bluntly replied before returning her attention to her computer.

"Sure...no problem, Maria," he stammered before sitting back at his desk.

Brandon had never seen Maria so upset. He wondered what was wrong and wanted to help Maria in any way he could, but he hesitated. He did not want to experience any awkwardness and reasoned that he had too much to do anyways. Besides, he figured that she would be back to her normal self soon enough.

* * *

"Just wait a couple of minutes Brandon. Mike will be right with you," Sheila mumbled while typing feverishly on her keyboard. Without looking in his direction, she motioned for him to have a seat with the tip of the pencil that dangled from her mouth.

Brandon was half way to a seat, when he made his way back to Sheila's desk. He figured that if anyone would know it was her. "Hey Sheila, you know what's going on with Maria? She looks off today."

Taking a rare break from nibbling on her pencil, Sheila pulled it out and looked at Brandon in amazement. "You don't know? You didn't hear about it? Human resources sent out a memo a couple of weeks ago."

Brandon shrugged his shoulders. "I never read those," he confessed nervously. "What's going on Sheila?"

"Her brother died in a car accident."

Brandon's jaw dropped. He tried to speak, but the words failed him. Finally, he managed to whisper, "Oh my God...Maria must be devastated."

"Well Yeah! No kidd'n," Sheila said shaking her head as she continued with her paper work.

Brandon walked to the nearest chair and sat down. He realized that, despite attending several meetings together, he never noticed anything different about her. 'My God,' he thought. 'How could I have been so insensitive?' He dropped his head towards the floor while closing his eyes. 'I can't believe that I didn't even notice.'

* * *

The remaining drops trickled to the bottom of the glass. Mike's desk was cleared except for the bottle of scotch and the glass he just emptied. Mike needed the drink. He took a deep breath and slowly nodded to himself. While putting the drink away, he buzzed his secretary. "Sheila, tell him to come in."

Brandon entered the room and took a seat.

"So what's up Mike? What did they say at the big meeting? What do they want us to do?"

"It's not exactly that simple, Brandon," Mike said. He paused and let out a big sigh before continuing. "It wasn't good Brandon. Not at all what I expected actually. But then again, with the new management in place there was no telling how they were going to react."

"What happened?" Brandon asked.

"Listen Brandon, I don't know how to tell you this. I really don't." For a moment Mike withdrew his normally intimidating eye contact. "I am just going to say it. We have to let you go kid. I'm sorry to be the one to tell you."

"You can't be serious?" Brandon said searching for a sign that Mike was playing a prank on him, but he could not find one. Brandon felt bewildered, and it was seconds before he looked up again, but when he did a single emotion pulsed through every cell of his body. Rage.

"What? What are you talking about Mike?" Brandon asked shaking his head.

"Brandon, take it easy," Mike said raising his hands trying to calm Brandon down. "You had to see this coming after last week. The deal. Someone has to take responsibility for it."

Brandon could not believe it. Mike was clearly the one who lost the deal. Clenching his fists, Brandon raised his voice as he stood up from the chair. "How about the person who messed it up? How about he takes the blame? I can't believe you can say this to me with a straight face Mike."

Mike didn't know what to say. He was surprised that Brandon hadn't even considered this happening. Still, even after being in the business for over twenty years, Mike couldn't help but feel a touch of guilt. "There was nothing I could do Brandon. I said I'm sorry, but don't blame me for life being the way it is," he replied firmly.

The finality of Mike's tone was like hearing the nail of his own coffin. Mike's voice faded into the background as Brandon aimlessly looked around the office. He saw Mike's moving lips, the tiny ornaments on the desk, and the golf clubs Mike had leant him just last week. In somewhat of a trance, Brandon turned to leave the office. He was halfway out of the room when the framed poster on the wall caught his attention. With the drowned out sound of Mike's voice still explaining himself in the background, Brandon sporadically read the words of the company mission statement.

Integrity...Honesty...Not just the bottom line...We value people...

'Nothing but empty words,' he thought to himself. He smiled with disdain and walked out of the office.

5

Brandon clutched the steering wheel as he reflected on the six long years spent with a company that just fired him for a mistake he never made.

The rush hour traffic was as intense as ever. The cars were bumper to bumper, and no one had moved for the past fifteen minutes. He sighed in frustration while looking around him. In a car to his left, a woman was so irritated by the traffic that she kept banging her head against the headrest. In the car directly behind her, there was a man who looked fast asleep. His jaw hung open while drool dribbled down the corner of his lips. Everywhere he looked, Brandon was startled to notice the same expression on so many faces. It was as if their eyes were searching for something more from life.

Like many people stuck in traffic that day, Brandon spent five days a week driving back and forth on those highways. He drove to the same building and had the same types of conversations for years. The same fears and insecurities continued to guide his life. He had done well for himself by most people's standards, yet he hadn't felt truly alive in years. Brandon could not help but wonder: 'Is this the life I imagined for myself?' That one innocent question triggered a flood of repressed thoughts and emotions.

They came in waves, one after the next. As they crashed against the shore of his being, Brandon found himself gripping the steering wheel more and more tightly. He remembered Maria and her eyes welling with tears as she looked at him for what seemed like an eternity. His failure to comfort her or even notice something was wrong for weeks sent a shudder down his spine. 'What have I become?' he thought. Maria's image wouldn't leave his mind. It kept haunting him and made him nauseous. Brandon recalled how she was the one who always helped him when he needed it the most and said to himself, 'I didn't even notice. I didn't even reach out when I could have.'

Maria's face dissolved from his mind's eye, only to be replaced with Edwin's image. With his long blond hair, the transition was smooth. Brandon was too ashamed to look Edwin in the eyes. He recalled how he had lied to Edwin. The truth was he gave up his great passion for climbing to pursue the successful career he just lost today. Then Edwin's words began to ring in his head, "I heard that you got over it." But, Brandon knew that he had not. Some parts of us never die.

The thought of Alisha provided some relief until he wondered how nervous she might be when he told her the news. He remembered the admiration of his friends and family, but all that meant nothing now because he no longer had his great job. He was a failure, and could not find comfort in anything. Brandon felt like the foundation of his life was crumbling beneath him. As he watched the structure collapse, he realized that the life he built for himself was as fragile as a house of cards.

6

Hours later, Brandon returned home a very different man. As he explained the events of his day to Alisha on the living room sofa, he had a calmness that alarmed her. Although he spoke of losing his job, he showed no signs of anger or remorse.

"I'm listening," she said while taking his hand in support.

"I am not going to look for another job Lish. I am going to do something I should have done a long time ago. Do you remember how I was going to climb Everest seven years back with Cameron and the crew?" Brandon asked. "Well, I am going to do it now."

"What?" Alisha exclaimed. This second piece of news was more shocking than the first. She didn't know what had gotten into

Brandon, but she knew this decision would drastically change their lives. "Brandon, what are you talking about?"

"I know it sounds crazy, but I gotta do this. I gotta climb her now."

"Sounds crazy? Alisha said as she yanked her hands away from his, "That's probably because it is crazy Brandon!"

"Alisha, this is something that has been eating away at me. It is something I have to do."

"So is that it? Did you want to talk about this or have you already decided?"

Brandon took a deep breath and firmly nodded his head.

"So that's it?" Alisha repeated. Looking down at the sofa, it became obvious that she said the words more to herself. "I can't believe he's going to climb again...I can't believe he's going to risk his life again."

"Hey," Brandon said quietly. "Lish. Try to understand. I need you with me on this one." Brandon looked into her eyes. "Just trust me. I have to do this."

Hearing his words, Alisha felt her will to stop him slipping away. She wanted him to be happy and fighting against the conviction in his voice made no sense to her. Yet, there were things she knew about Brandon and climbing that even he did not know.

"NO!" she said as she stood up and turned away from him. He could see her wiping her eyes quickly. "No you don't have to do this, Brandon. Do you really believe climbing Everest is going to solve your problems? That's a total myth. That's what you never understood. You won't be happy even if you get there. You never were! I remember your climbing days. I remember how after every mountain you conquered, it wasn't long before you'd be looking for another one. You were just never satisfied."

Brandon was stung by her words. "And what about here, Lish? What's so different about this life you speak so highly of? No matter how much we have or achieve – the money, the promotions, the next step towards enlightenment – when will it ever be enough Lish? When will we ever feel good enough?" His words surprised even himself. Although he said them mainly in defense, he spoke with a clarity that could not be denied.

Alisha turned to face Brandon, "Well then it doesn't matter, does it? Whether you're here or there you won't find lasting satisfaction anywhere. At least have the guts to face life. You can't keep running away Brandon. There is nothing up there at the top of the mountain. There never was, and you know it." Knowing how much this would hurt Brandon, she had promised herself never to share these thoughts with him. Yet, in her desperation to keep their lives together she lashed out at the same heart that she had so often sheltered from life's blows.

Brandon didn't know how to respond. The feelings that he felt from the drive home stayed with him, and he didn't care if he had the words to defend it. "Well, at least there is one thing I do know. I feel alive when I climb those mountains. But here, here I've been feeling more and more dead with every passing day. Damn it! There's got to be more to life than this!"

There was nothing left to say. Exhausted, they remained in silence for a moment.

Though Alisha said the words calmly, it took all her strength to say them. "I can't do this Brandon. I'll always love you, but I can't go back to living that life again. If you go, you go without me." She turned and slowly walked towards the bedroom.

Brandon was left on the sofa stunned by her final comment. He never expected his decision might lead to their breakup. Unable to imagine his life without the woman he loved, Brandon watched the final card in his life come crashing down. He heard the bedroom door close from behind him. As he let his body sink into the sofa, he experienced a strange feeling. It was the sensation of falling.

7

At six thousand meters, the view was breathtaking. Surrounded by clouded, white mountain peaks, Cameron and Brandon began to fully appreciate why the Tibetans referred to Everest as *Jomolungma*, the goddess of the world. With every step they grew convinced that if there was a heaven on earth, this was it.

Cameron watched Brandon from below. They had been training together for a year. Since Brandon left the sport, Cameron never found a partner he got along with and trusted as much. In fact it was Cameron who had vouched for him to join the six man expedition up Everest. Cameron watched as Brandon expertly led their ascent up what was known in some climbing circles as Devil's Ramp. Climbing the north face was once considered a novel task, but over the past couple of decades, Everest had seen a fair share of traffic. Still, no amount of wear and tear up this ramp prevented it from living up to its reputation for having one of the most dangerous drops.

'Brandon needs to get some protection,' Cameron thought to himself while watching Brandon climb. 'One more and we're in the clear for the day.'

Brandon's hands searched the rocks for a crack. It had been a good twenty feet since Brandon anchored, and he knew he had to do it soon. The trouble was that there were scarcely any cracks, and the powdery snow made it virtually impossible to create one himself.

Sensing the urgency, Brandon's focus intensified. With his right arm outstretched he felt a large enough crack within his reach. He took only a small step, but that was enough for him to lose control. Brandon struggled to hold on as the unstable rock collapsed beneath him. He gasped as he felt himself slipping off the ramp. With only one hand holding on, the rest of his body dangled in midair. In desperation, Brandon reached for something else to hold onto, but it was no use. The icy rocks were too slippery. His arm convulsed uncontrollably as he struggled to hold on. Brandon looked around himself and saw no hope. Surrendering to the force of gravity, he fell. The sensation felt familiar.

8

Brandon felt a wave of serenity flow through his body before opening his eyes. He looked up to see a beautiful bird flying gracefully through the blue skies. It had light orange feathers with shining eyes. Brandon was startled to watch it morph into a human being with wings. It kept interchanging between the two forms. He was captivated by its mystery and was disappointed to watch it disappear into the clouds.

As Brandon slowly sat up, the memory of falling flashed back into his head like a terrifying nightmare. He was also confused to find himself lying on a bed surrounded by dozens of gadgets and monitors. Looking to his right, he was startled to see two faces that had been staring at him the whole time. One belonged to a man seated in front of a computer screen wearing a lab coat and glasses. The other belonged to a female who stood closer, by the foot of the bed, wearing a dark navy suit. She spoke first.

"Brandon, welcome to F-Max. My name is Malaya," she said while extending her hand in an inviting welcome.

Her friendly demeanor helped Brandon feel relaxed enough to regain his composure. Shaking Malaya's hand, Brandon asked, "F-Max? What is this place?"

Malaya was used to explaining this and spoke with a mastered reassurance. "I know this may be hard to believe Brandon, but you are in a subconscious realm. F-Max is an organization that specializes in freeing the human mind and heart. The human psyche is fascinating. Not many people understand it, let alone realize they are imprisoned by it. But, that has been our area of research for the last few centuries. We have access to whatever information we need, and we have complete authorization to guide people wherever we see fit."

"Guide? What do you mean?"

"Guide them to completely accept themselves and to live life on their own terms." Nestor broke in excitedly from behind Malaya. "Things like insights that come out of nowhere, books that you come upon at the right time in your life, and coincidences that make you more in tune with yourself. They all come from different divisions of our organization."

"Right," Malaya said.

"Wait. Are you trying to tell me that I am inside my mind?" Brandon asked.

"Not your mind. A subconscious realm," Malaya corrected.

"Does that mean I'm dead?" Brandon asked.

Realizing that she did not have adequate time to explain these things, Malaya got to the point. "Fortunately not, but I will be honest with you, your chances are slim. Take a look for yourself." Malaya raised a remote control in her hand and drew Brandon's attention to the monitor in front of the bed. Brandon saw himself lying unconscious in the snow. "Your leg broke while you fell, and hypothermia will become fatal once the sun sets," she continued.

"Will I make it?" Brandon asked.

"That depends mostly on you. Your friend Cameron and some locals are working on rescuing you, but that will be futile if you lose your will to live. Brandon, you see that dial on the left side, the one barely reaching level two?"

"Yes."

"Well that dial is measuring your will to live. Now, as you can see, you are not doing too well out there. We figure you are going to need a reading of at least eight to survive this," said Malaya.

"How do I do that?" Brandon asked.

"You will have to genuinely believe that your life is worth living."

"What's the point?" Brandon replied disheartened. "Everything I had left to live for was in that climb."

Malaya started to speak, but refrained herself. She nodded acknowledging her own limits. "Brandon, I would like to introduce you to Doctor Nestor, our chief scientist here at F-Max. He will take over from here. You have much to discuss."

"It is a pleasure to meet you," said Nestor.

Malaya gently placed her hand on Brandon's. "I hope you will keep an open mind and thoroughly consider what he says. There is one thing you should know. We are not in the business of saving people's lives. We only brought you here because you are close to something, something you have been searching for, for a long time. We would like to help you understand what that is. Good luck Brandon," Malaya said while looking at him warmly. She then turned to leave the room.

Brandon looked at Nestor somewhat bewildered. "What exactly is she talking about? What am I close to?"

Taking a deep breath while pushing his glasses in, Nestor began the conversation he had been waiting to have for years.

"Brandon, sit back and relax. Before you can understand what Malaya is alluding to, I need to give you some background information. You see Brandon, the moment you were born was the start of a process that has gradually stripped you of your freedom to feel good about yourself. As an infant you sought love from your parents who would rush to your aid every time you cried. But, as you grew older you found that to gain their love and affection, you needed to conform to their hopes and expectations of you. Your parents were particularly pleased when you did well in school or won a competition. Your main reason for striving to accomplish so much as a child was to see the pride in their eyes when they congratulated your success. Unconsciously, you pushed yourself to do all the things that were expected of you because you wanted their love and affection.

"This need to please your parents has been a strong influence throughout your early life because you believed that your parent's love was necessary for you to fully love and accept yourself. When they were proud of you, you gave yourself permission to accept yourself.

"The expectations of various social forces including your culture, friends, and workplace have also influenced your ideas of what you need to do in order to be acceptable. You grew up with thoughts of how you could gain love and respect by being financially secure, successful, or even adventurous. The media has also shaped your beliefs of what is beautiful and how you need to look to feel good about yourself. How am I doing so far?" Nestor asked reminding himself to take a breath.

"It's all making sense, but I don't quite understand what you're trying to get at," replied Brandon.

"Brandon, all of these ideas have been reinforcing a single belief within you that has been dominating your experience of life. This belief is that *you are not worthy of love and acceptance as you are*. In other words, you need to prove your worth before you can feel good about yourself. I am trying to make you realize that most of the things you pursued in life were really an attempt to show that you deserve love and acceptance. To illustrate the point, let me use a recent example. Remember meeting Edwin on the night of your thirty-fifth birthday party, and how you lied to him about your real reason for not climbing Everest?"

"Of course I remember," replied Brandon.

"Why do you think you lied to him?"

"I dunno...I guess I didn't want him to think any less of me. I was afraid that if he found out the truth he might start to look at me totally differently."

"Exactly. Like most people, deep down you share a strong need to have the approval of those around you. You were afraid to tell Edwin the truth because you needed his acceptance before you could accept yourself. But, it is important to understand that deep down you are not looking for Edwin's acceptance or anyone else's for that matter. You are really looking for your own. However, you have been conditioned to believe that you cannot give that acceptance to yourself unless certain people accept you first. Trying to gain the approval of others is just one of the many ways you seek to prove that you are worthy of love. It is one of the many conditions you must fulfill before you can accept yourself."

Brandon was quiet as he reflected on what had been said. "I see how this is happening in my life, but I can't believe that this need to prove my worth is behind almost everything I do."

"What would you say if I told you that even this climb is related to your need for approval?"

"That is where you are wrong" Brandon jumped in, "I'm not doing this to gain anyone's approval. In fact most people I know don't want me to do this climb. I even lost the one woman whose approval meant more than anything to me," Brandon said.

"Yes, I know Brandon. You did not do this climb for anyone else's approval, you did it to get your own approval. You made these sacrifices to prove to yourself that you could do it, that you could be a success. But, conquering the mountain is not really what you seek. It is the feeling of being loved and accepted by none other than yourself. Since you do not believe that you are worthy of this love as you are, your life will always revolve around trying to give yourself proof. Think about it Brandon, even if you do get to the top, how long will your joy last? How long will it be before you are back out there trying to prove your worth again?"

Brandon gasped as he heard Nestor's words. "So, Alisha was right?"

"You both were right in your own way," Nestor replied.

Brandon took a moment to digest what he heard before commenting. "But, isn't proving my worth what pushes me to achieve things? If we don't try to prove our worth how can there ever be progress in our lives?"

"There is a lot more that you need to explore before you can fully understand the answers to your questions, Brandon. But, I can tell you now that needing to prove your worth is not the only way to motivate yourself, and it certainly is not the most effective way. In fact, it is the belief that you are not worthy of love as you are, that is behind the stress, fear, and self-consciousness that drain your energy. To make matters worse, as long as you have this belief you will exhaust yourself trying to fulfill the conditions you have placed on the love you seek. You will soon discover how all of this is happening at the expense of knowing and expressing yourself. You will also come to understand how this belief is preventing you from experiencing the love and freedom you truly long for."

There was a long silence as Brandon withdrew into deep thought. Nestor waited until Brandon's attention returned before he continued. "If it makes you feel any better, this is the way most people live. Even Edwin at the party was craving your acceptance so that he could feel better about himself. Almost everyone is searching for reasons to feel worthy of love. And yet, so many people are beginning to realize that, no matter what they do, it never seems to be enough."

"Yes, that's exactly it. It never seems to be enough," Brandon said shaking his head slowly. "But, it doesn't help me to know that other people are living this way. The problem is still there, and I'm just so tired of it. So tired of leading this kind of life...but now what? Now that I'm aware of this belief, what can I do?" Brandon asked.

"That is the fun part," Nestor said with a beaming smile. He sensed Brandon's enthusiasm for life returning, and when the dial showed a reading of seven, Nestor was inspired to speak with greater passion. "Your transformation lies in challenging the fundamental belief that you are not worthy of love as you are."

"But, how do I do this?" Brandon asked.

"Patience Brandon. You will be shown a way. And when this transformation takes place, you will no longer need to climb another mountain again."

"What do you mean?"

"Let us just say that you will realize the true relationship between you and the mountain, between you and any other goal you have ever strived to conquer."

"And what's that?" Brandon asked.

"That you are B – "

Nestor was interrupted by a soft beep from the monitor. The dial showed a reading of eight. Nestor closed his eyes momentarily and nodded to himself. He turned to Brandon and looked at him with a smile. It was the last thing Brandon saw as the room slowly dissolved from view, and he heard Nestor's final words.

"You will see Brandon. Soon enough, you will see…"

9

As Brandon peered out the window, he took a moment to appreciate how fortunate he was to be alive. If it were not for the help of Tarak, a local Sherpa, Brandon would have died the night of the fall. Though a complete stranger, Tarak risked his life to rescue Brandon.

Brandon got up from his bed in pain and with the support of crutches. That afternoon, Brandon decided he would take his first tour of Tarak's home. Until then, he had spent most of his time in bed. Tarak was working in the kitchen, and Brandon could already smell the aroma of lunch being prepared.

Tarak had done a remarkable job of furnishing his small home. Its cozy ambiance was a perfect blend of comfort and function. Soaking in the atmosphere while adjusting to the feeling of walking, Brandon ambled over to a wooden chair. He took a seat and perused through a modest collection of books resting on a small table. Most of the books were written in the native Tibetan language. Brandon was about to abandon his search for something to read when he noticed a stack of loosely bound pages that had the look of a recently finished manuscript. He casually reached over to pick it up and gasped when he saw the front cover. Up until then he thought his conversation with Doctor Nestor was another hallucination from the herbal painkillers. Looking down at the photograph on the front cover, his heart raced. It was a still-shot of the same mysterious bird he saw at F-Max before it morphed into a human.

"Tarak!" he called out while hobbling towards the kitchen. Resting on his crutches he pointed at the manuscript and asked, "Where did you get this?"

"You are up. Very good. Do you like place?"

"Yes, it's beautiful. Very nice." Brandon said giving the requisite politeness. "Where did you get this?" he repeated.

"This? Four or five days back, man come here...late night, lost in mountain. Crazy man. He come alone all the way! He stay here one night. Next day, he leave early morning. He leave this behind," replied Tarak.

"May I read it?" Brandon asked as Tarak added some final seasoning to the pot of freshly made food.

Tarak nodded indicating that he had no use for it. "Yes, yes. Why not? Don't know address of man, so what to do," said Tarak shrugging his shoulders with a wooden spoon in one hand. "Funny man. Very funny. He talk much. Glasses always coming off nose," said Tarak.

"Brandon, you're up, mate!" Cameron said as he ducked slightly to enter the kitchen doorway. Being a good friend he stayed back to support Brandon through the recovery. "This is great. You must be feeling good today. Hey, how are the crutches? Not like they make them at home I assume?"

"No, but I'm not complaining. They work. I'm happy with that," Brandon replied though still preoccupied with the manuscript in his hand.

Cameron nodded in agreement. He then turned to Tarak and asked, "You ready to get the medicine?"

"Yes, we go right away," Tarak replied while pouring a plate of food for Brandon. "Your lunch is on table."

"Thanks Tarak. You are too good to me," replied Brandon.

"We'll be back in an hour or so Brandon. Try to get some rest," Cameron said as they walked out the door.

Brandon hobbled to the first chair he could find. Lunchtime normally found him starving, but the manuscript that now rested on his lap consumed all his attention. He looked down again at the cover. There could be no mistaking that it was the same bird. Brandon recalled his experience with Nestor and smiled. He remembered their conversation and relived the anticipation he felt just before Nestor disappeared from view. Struck by wonder, he took a moment to gaze out the window and appreciate the panoramic view of the surrounding Himalayan mountain range. Slowly looking back to the manuscript, he let out a deep sigh, and turned to the first page...

THE
MANUSCRIPT

THE JOURNEY AHEAD

You are about to embark on a journey like none you have taken before. On this journey, you will leave behind every idea of what you are supposed to be and uncover who you really are. In the pages to follow, you will dive beneath the surface of your everyday experiences to understand how a belief you did not choose is severely limiting you. But the journey will not end there. As you read on, you will explore an alternative that will empower you to break free from these limitations and reinvent the possibilities in your life.

THE STORY WE ALL SHARE

Before we begin, it is important to understand that, despite our differences, we all share a remarkably similar past. During our most impressionable years, we have been taught by our surroundings which thoughts and behaviors are acceptable. This education shaped how we perceive the world and ourselves. Throughout these formative years, we inherited a destructive belief that dominates our experience of life to this day. This belief is:

I am not worthy of love and acceptance as I am.

Although at first glance, this belief may seem harmless, you will soon realize its far-reaching implications and the oppressive role it can play in your life. You will also learn how this single belief leads to twelve major psychological addictions that make it impossible for you to find the satisfaction you seek.

To truly understand this belief, we must go back to the very beginning of our lives. This belief entered our minds as a result of many conventions we took for granted and accepted as normal.

When we were born, we found ourselves completely dependent on our parents. They provided nourishment for our bodies, and their love gave us the emotional security to explore our new world. In the beginning, we were perfect to our parents, and there was nothing they wanted more than to shower us with their love and affection. This love was given to us with very few, if any, strings attached.

As we grew older, however, experiencing our parent's love became increasingly difficult. Though our parents may have had the best of intentions, they often made the mistake of withdrawing their love and affection as a means of getting us to behave the way they wanted. As little children, we learned that gaining their love and acceptance required fulfilling their expectations of us. Whenever we failed to meet these expectations, we were considered "bad" boys or girls. There was nothing we wished to avoid more than the disappointed faces of our parents. For it was only when they loved us that we felt lovable. Only when they accepted us could we accept ourselves. As a result, we learned that we were only acceptable when we met the expectations of our parents. We began to believe that we were only worthy of love when we proved it, and not worthy of love as we are. In this first crucial relationship with our surroundings, the foundation for this belief was laid. And it would be reinforced wherever we went.

At school, our interactions with peers taught us how we needed to behave to fit in. Depending on the social circle we wished to be a part of, we quickly learned how we should dress, talk, and even think. From our interactions with teachers, we learned that those who did well academically, artistically or athletically deserved praise and affection. While those who did not were usually treated like they were mediocre. The underlying message at school was loud and clear: we were not worthy of love and acceptance as we were. We were only worthy when we proved it by living up to the expectations of our surroundings.

In addition, our exposure to the media and other social influences played a powerful role in reinforcing this belief in our minds. These influences continue to affect us by imposing their own expectations of what we need to acquire, achieve or become before we can feel completely acceptable. All of these social forces combined have drilled the same message deep into the core of our psyches. As adults, how we each strive to prove our worth may differ, but the fundamental belief behind our efforts remains the same – I am not worthy of love as I am.

This journey is about understanding the oppressive role this belief plays in your life and how you can break free from it.

THE PROCESS

The Born on the Mountaintop journey has been divided into four distinct sections: (1) Awareness, (2) Mind Transformation (3) Manifestation and (4) Keeping the Commitment.

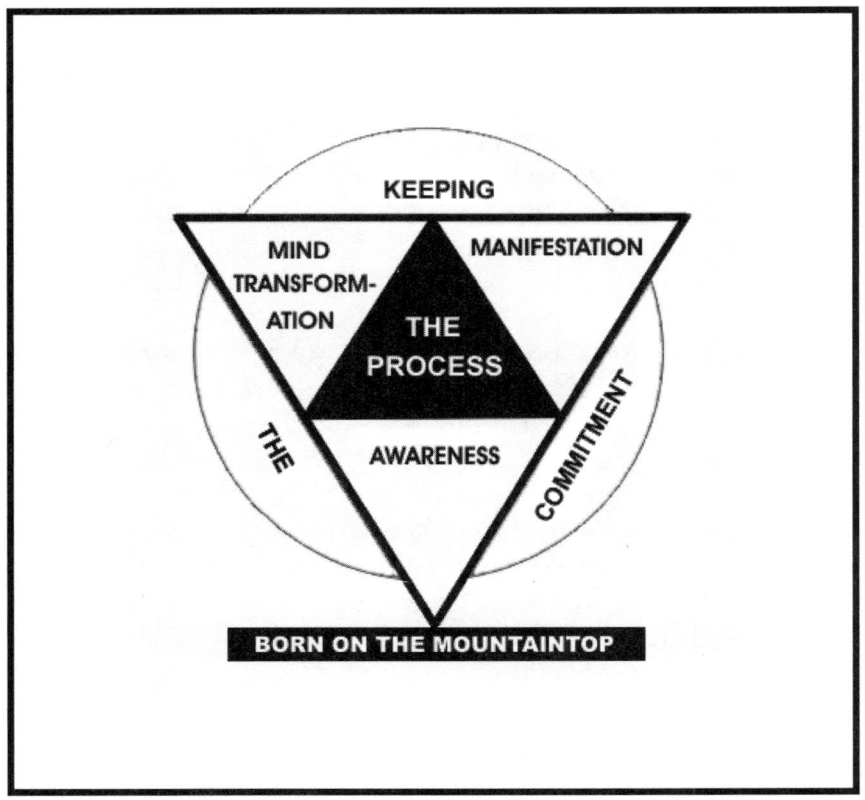

Awareness:

The first step to reclaiming your personal freedom is to understand how that freedom has been limited. That is why you will begin the Awareness section by learning about the Conditional Love State (CLS). The CLS is a way of living based on the belief that "I am not worthy of love and acceptance as I am." The CLS affects each of us differently and presents itself in our lives as twelve powerful psychological addictions. To help you understand how these addictions are specifically influencing your life, you will be introduced to diagnostic tools and innovative exercises that encourage self-reflection.

After acquiring this deepened awareness of yourself, you will explore how to break free from the limitations of the CLS. In this stage of the journey, you will be introduced to an exciting and revolutionary way of thinking. During these exercises, you will tap into a part of yourself that is no longer burdened by insecurity and fear. You will also be able to access your deeper motivations and understand who you really are, not who you have been taught to be by your surroundings.

Mind Transformation:

The CLS has been a part of your life since you were born, and it has resulted in deep-rooted emotional and behavioral patterns. Given this, how can you move away from this state and build a life based on new insights? The next three sections have been designed to answer this question. The Mind Transformation section will teach you how to break free from the CLS through transforming your thoughts and emotions. The tools you learn here will help you build a relationship with yourself based on love and freedom.

Manifestation:

In Manifestation, you will learn how to apply the transformation of your thinking into the realm of action. This section is divided into two parts. In the first part, you will learn how to reclaim your freedom in your day-to-day activities. Here you will explore how you can start doing and saying the things you really want. The second part will empower you to develop more harmonious relationships with people in your life. When you finish this section, you will understand how your behavior may actually be inhibiting people close to you. Whether you apply these insights to your partner, children, parents, or close friends, you will learn to develop relationships based on a foundation of real understanding and free from the expectations that prevent us from appreciating each other.

Keeping The Commitment:

Throughout the Born on the Mountaintop journey, you will discover many important tools. Which of the tools you choose to apply to your life is your decision. Whatever you choose, it is crucial to have a strategy in place that will ensure you keep your commitments to yourself. This last section was developed to help you keep the fire of your motivation alive. It will reveal the most common traps people fall into when trying to fulfill their goals and how you can avoid them. Most importantly, you will learn innovative techniques that will help you honor your new commitments to yourself, while enjoying the process.

How To Approach This Journey

Although you will gain many insights from simply reading this book, it is highly recommended that you take the time to stop and do the exercises as they arise. By investing this time you will appreciate the extent to which these issues are affecting you. It is also important to do the exercises in the order they appear because they are intimately related and build on each other. Ultimately, the quality of your experience will depend on your willingness to challenge existing beliefs and be honest with yourself. Remember, the tools in the book were designed to help you learn about yourself. No one needs to see them except you. Most importantly enjoy the journey. After all, you are about to dive into an exploration of one of the most fascinating wonders of the world – you.

Part 1

AWARENESS

The Gateway to Freedom

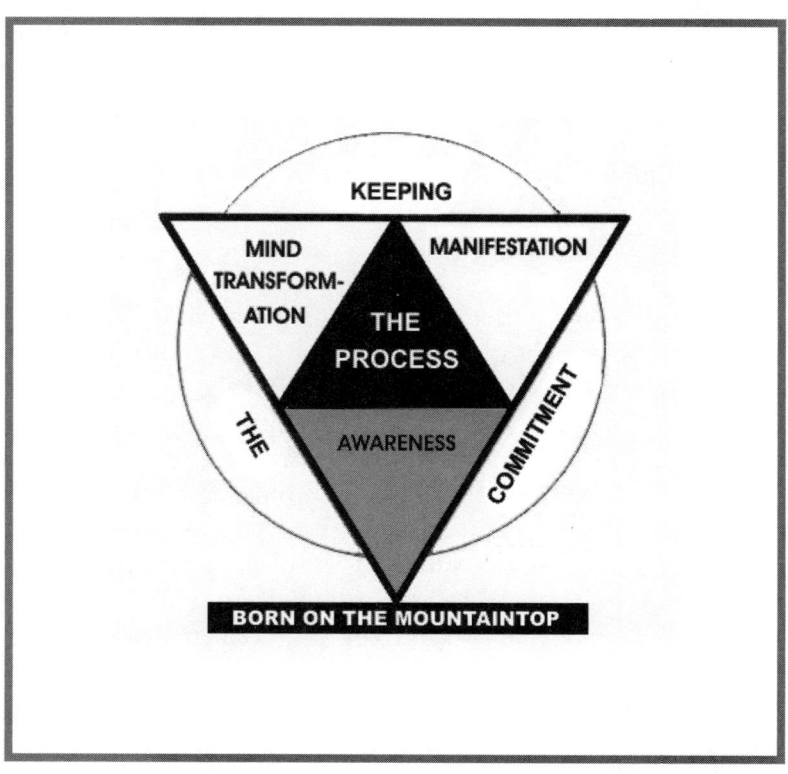

Awareness

When we're deluded there's a world to escape.
When we're aware, there's nothing to escape.

BODHIDHARMA

Since the day you were born, society has reinforced the notion that you are not worthy of love as you are. We have already explored how this has occurred, but we have hardly begun to examine how this single belief shapes our lives and what other alternatives may exist. The Born on the Mountaintop journey begins with awareness because it would not make sense to start anywhere else. You need to become aware of where you are before you can decide where you want to go or if, in fact, you want to go anywhere at all. The following scenario will help illustrate the importance of awareness.

Looking Under The Hood

Imagine you go to see your car mechanic after a long time. How would you feel if, without even taking a moment to examine what was wrong with your car, he immediately opened the hood and started replacing random parts? Would you be confused? Shocked maybe? You are about to embark on a process of understanding something far more complex than a car – your thoughts and feelings. While doing this, you definitely do not want to make the mechanic's mistake of rushing to make changes. The Awareness section is placed right at the onset of this journey because it gives you the opportunity to thoroughly understand where your fear, insecurity, self-consciousness and stress are coming from. Like the mechanic, people often tend to skip this step and rush to find solutions without a deepened understanding of why these emotions are arising. This usually happens because we want to see results. But, how can we hope to move beyond something we do not fully understand? Incomplete awareness leads to incomplete analysis, which can only lead to incomplete solutions. That is why so much of the Awareness section is devoted to understanding what is going on within you before venturing to find a solution.

No matter what you do, if you do not take the time to understand a problem, you can never be effective in overcoming it. On the other hand, a deepened awareness of the problem gives you an incredible power over your life. Uncertainty dissolves, as clarity emerges. The problem is seen in its entirety, and what needs to be done becomes apparent. This awareness gives you an appreciation of your options and empowers you with the capacity to choose.

The purpose of the Awareness Section is to:

1) Instill an awareness of how the belief that "you are not worthy of love as you are" is severely limiting your freedom. To help achieve this, you will be applying the following tools:

>*The CLS Survey*
>*The CLS Inventory*
>*Confirming the Addictions You Have*
>*Recalling Addictive Behavior*
>*Breaking Down Your Addictions*
>*Experiencing Withdrawal*

2) Introduce and explore an entirely new way of experiencing life in complete freedom. To facilitate this process you will use the following tools:

>*Exploring the ULS*
>*Weighing Your Options*

3) Empower you with the freedom to choose your own life experiences.

Taking the time to reflect on these tools will reveal the bigger picture like never before, and allow you to discover parts of yourself that are waiting to unfold. So sit back, relax, and give yourself the psychological space to see what is going on under your hood.

A Spirit Of Non-Judgmental Exploration

As you delve into your innermost thoughts and feelings, you will discover many things about yourself. Some you may like and some you may not, but it is very important to avoid the tendency to criticize yourself along the way. Not only will such self-judgment prevent you from understanding what is going on within, but it will also make the journey itself a very uncomfortable experience. Instead, we encourage you to approach this section in a spirit of exploration. These exercises were designed to help you understand your inner world, and what could be more exciting than discovering who you are?

The CLS Survey

It is time to begin now with an exercise called The CLS Survey. This survey was developed to help deepen your awareness of the thoughts and emotions you experience. As you fill in the survey, please keep in mind that there are no "right" or "wrong" answers. The purpose of the survey is to open your mind to the topics of exploration to follow.

To complete the survey, simply check whether you *Agree* or *Disagree* with the statements listed. The survey is meant to be done quickly and candidly. So try to answer with your honest, gut response. If you feel that the statement only applies sometimes, still check *Agree*.

Determine whether you agree or disagree with each of the following statements.

	AGREE	DISAGREE
1) When I walk into a room full of strangers, at times I am self-conscious about how others perceive me.	☐	☐
2) I believe that being in a relationship will make my life more fulfilled.	☐	☐
3) I experience a sense of guilt when I am not as spiritual as I would like to be.	☐	☐
4) What certain people think of me can affect the way I feel about myself.	☐	☐
5) I would consider myself to be a failure if I do not do something extraordinary with my life or find something I am passionate about.	☐	☐
6) I get frustrated when things are not put back in their proper place.	☐	☐
7) I am proud of the number of partners or sexual experiences I have had.	☐	☐

	AGREE	DISAGREE

8) I feel better about myself when someone beautiful finds me attractive. ☐ ☐

9) I get disappointed whenever I don't accomplish enough in a day. ☐ ☐

10) I don't enjoy playing a game when I am losing. ☐ ☐

11) I spend a lot of time thinking about what's wrong in the world and this upsets me. ☐ ☐

12) I am quick to find flaws in the people I interact with. ☐ ☐

13) I have difficulty being content with my work unless it is nearly perfect. ☐ ☐

14) My sense of spirituality makes me feel more evolved than some of the people I meet. ☐ ☐

15) I admire people who are successful or famous. ☐ ☐

16) What other people think of my partner, family, or friends is important to me. ☐ ☐

17) I feel better about myself when I achieve what I set out to do in my day. ☐ ☐

18) I can get jealous of, or feel insecure around, people who are better than me in certain areas of my life. ☐ ☐

19) I feel guilty about people in other parts of the world who are suffering needlessly. ☐ ☐

20) I get bothered by the way certain people behave and criticize them often. ☐ ☐

21) I would feel better about myself if I had more money. ☐ ☐

AWARENESS

	AGREE	DISAGREE
22) I feel bad when someone I care about is unhappy with me.	☐	☐
23) I want to sleep with as many attractive people as I can.	☐	☐
24) I feel disappointed in myself when I get angry or jealous.	☐	☐
25) I tend to get upset with myself when I make a mistake.	☐	☐
26) I am uncomfortable or self-conscious wearing a swimsuit by the pool.	☐	☐
27) I can get upset with my family members, friends, or partner when they do not meet my expectations of them.	☐	☐
28) I have an idea of how I want my body to look and have difficulty being happy with myself unless it looks that way.	☐	☐
29) At times I hesitate to take on new challenges because I am afraid of what others might think.	☐	☐
30) Sometimes I do not share my feelings, when I am with my partner or a potential partner.	☐	☐
31) I feel guilty when I waste time.	☐	☐
32) Sometimes I can feel emotionally drained while trying to make a positive difference in the world.	☐	☐
33) There are times when I get embarrassed by the things my partner, family members, or friends do.	☐	☐
34) I like it when people notice my nice car, clothes, or other possessions.	☐	☐

	AGREE	DISAGREE

35) I can feel anxious whenever I am unable to figure out the reason behind the events in my life. ☐ ☐

36) Sometimes when I criticize others it helps me feel a little better about myself. ☐ ☐

37) Sometimes I hesitate to share my thoughts because I am afraid of what other people might think. ☐ ☐

38) I compare myself with others and this can either positively or negatively affect how I feel about myself. ☐ ☐

39) When I am with my partner or a potential partner, sometimes I feel a need to impress him/her. ☐ ☐

40) Sometimes I get so caught up in trying to help others that I neglect to take good care of myself. ☐ ☐

41) At times, I feel guilty when I have sex. ☐ ☐

42) Having prestige in society is important to me. ☐ ☐

43) At times, I stop myself from doing things because I am afraid I might make a mistake. ☐ ☐

44) I feel that I need to be good in bed in order to feel good about myself. ☐ ☐

45) Sometimes I feel bad when people do not approve of my family or friends. ☐ ☐

46) I believe that I should have "pure" thoughts and/or avoid negative thinking patterns. ☐ ☐

47) I work hard to look a certain way. ☐ ☐

AWARENESS

AGREE DISAGREE

48) I try to be the best at what I do. ☐ ☐

49) I have trouble relaxing or doing nothing. ☐ ☐

50) (If married or in a relationship) I would
    be heart-broken if my relationship ended. ☐ ☐

We will assess the results of the survey shortly, but first let us begin our exploration of the Conditional Love State (CLS), a way of living that will be the focal point of the next few exercises.

THE CONDITIONAL LOVE STATE (CLS)

Think of a time when you felt really good about yourself. What was it that allowed you to feel this way? If you are like most people, you probably had to give yourself some reason to justify feeling good. Now think of a time when other people expressed their approval of you. How did you gain this approval? In this case also, you likely had to give them a reason or meet some expectation in order to get their approval. Whether from ourselves or other people, the love and acceptance we have received has mostly been limited to the times we proved ourselves worthy of it. This is how we are used to receiving love – by earning it – and it is best described as the Conditional Love State (CLS). Understanding this state in detail is one of the most important steps of the Awareness section.

To put it simply, the CLS requires you to fulfill conditions before you can feel completely worthy of love and acceptance. The possible conditions you can place on feeling worthy of love are endless and vary for each of us. For example, these conditions could entail being successful, being productive, finding a life-partner, or appearing a certain way. They may also include becoming a better person, helping the world be a safer place, or reaching a state of enlightenment. Although there is nothing wrong with pursuing these goals, when they become conditions for loving or accepting yourself, you find yourself in the CLS.

At first glance, you may not notice anything strange or harmful about the CLS. As mentioned earlier, this is how most of us are used to experiencing love. Yet, despite how much we take this experience for granted, it is the cause of most of our limitations. In fact, as you begin to explore how the CLS affects you, you will uncover the destructive role it can play in almost every aspect of your life, including how you think, feel, and behave. If you want to reclaim your freedom, you must begin with understanding the CLS. To do this, it is essential to review the following features of this state:

The CLS is based on the central belief: "I am not worthy of love and acceptance as I am."

This central belief can be worded in other ways as well. For example, it could also be described as:

"I need to prove that I deserve love and acceptance."
"I am not good enough as I am."
"I need a reason to love and accept myself."

Regardless of how it is expressed, this central belief prevents people in the CLS from completely accepting themselves as they are. It is a **central** belief because when we have this belief our lives revolve around proving our worthiness of love and acceptance.

The CLS and its central belief are strongly reinforced by our environment.

Few of us can avoid the CLS because we have all been born into a world that deeply supports its central belief. In fact, most of us have not been given a reason to believe otherwise. Almost every message we have received has told us that we need to be something else to be more acceptable.

We have already looked at the way we receive this message from our parents and schooling. The media is also among the most powerful of social influences. Messages from television, movies and magazines set the trend of what is deemed appropriate and what is not. In subtle, yet very effective ways, they reinforce the CLS in our minds. The most effective advertisements are those that succeed in associating their product to our sense of self-esteem. The best advertisers do not sell services or products. They sell self-love and self-acceptance. As a result, many ads reinforce the idea that buying what they have to offer will make us feel more worthy of the love and acceptance we long for.

When we examine the forces of our upbringing, education, the people we interact with, and the media it becomes clear that the central belief of the CLS is unconsciously being reinforced wherever we go.

In the CLS we make a contract with ourselves.

In a legal contract there are a set of rules, usually referred to as "terms and conditions," that must be followed in order for the contract to stay valid. In the CLS, we make a similar contract with ourselves. In this contract we determine the conditions that must be met before we can feel acceptable in our own eyes. Although the contract is not made consciously, the message we tell ourselves is clear: "I cannot fully accept myself unless I fulfill certain conditions." Some of these conditions come from the world around us, and others may come from our own personal convictions. In either case, when the conditions are not met the contract is breached, and we experience the emotional pain of being unworthy of love and acceptance.

The CLS presents itself in our lives as addictions.

Love and acceptance are our deepest psychological needs. In fact, most psychologists would agree that we need to feel acceptable in order to be healthy and function well in society. Since there are a set of conditions that must be met before we can feel the love and acceptance we long for, fulfilling these conditions becomes essential to our well-being. We do not just want to fulfill them, we need to. With this in mind, you can begin to appreciate one of the most fascinating aspects of the CLS – Addictions.

> **In the CLS you become addicted to fulfilling the conditions that prove your worth because you have been led to believe this is the only way to experience the love you long for.**

Although the term addiction seems strong, you will soon receive a more detailed explanation of why the behaviors in the CLS are addictive. For now, let us take a look at what the CLS Survey revealed about your possible addictions.

LOVE, ACCEPTANCE, AND SELF-WORTH

When it comes to understanding the CLS, some people can relate to the struggle for self-acceptance, while others can relate more to the struggle for self-love or establishing their self-worth. That is why, in the context of addictions, we have used the words "love," "worth," and "acceptance" interchangeably in this book.

Taking Inventory Of Your Addictions

Although there are many ways in which we attempt to prove that we are worthy of love, most of them relate to a major Conditional Love State (CLS) Addiction. The CLS Survey you completed earlier helps to uncover which of the twelve major CLS Addictions you possibly have. These addictions are listed in the left hand column of the table provided on the next page. By matching your responses in the CLS Survey with the addictions listed, you will be able to determine your possible addictions. For each addiction, if you agreed to one or more of its related statements, check the box under the *My Possible Addictions* column. For example, if you agreed to statement number 29 you would check the Acceptance of Others box under the My Possible Addictions column.

Just because you agreed with certain statements does not necessarily mean that you have the related addiction. You can only confirm which addictions you have after reading the detailed descriptions that will be provided for each addiction. For this reason, ignore the *My Confirmed Addictions* column for now. You will be invited to confirm which addictions you have after learning more about each of them.

A Helpful Tip

To avoid having to flip back and forth between these pages and the CLS survey, it is highly recommended that you review the CLS survey and write down all the numbers of the statements you agreed with on a separate page. Then come back to this CLS Inventory and check off your possible addictions.

AWARENESS

ADDICTIONS	RELATED STATEMENTS FROM THE SURVEY	MY POSSIBLE ADDICTIONS	MY CONFIRMED ADDICTIONS
Acceptance of Others	If you agree to statements 1, 4, 22, 29 or 37	☐	☐
Perfection	If you agree to statements 6, 13, 24, 25 or 43	☐	☐
Appearance	If you agree to statements 8, 26, 28 or 47	☐	☐
Success	If you agree to statements 5, 15, 21, 34 or 42	☐	☐
"The One"	If you agree to statements 2, 30, 39 or 50	☐	☐
Save the World	If you agree to statements 11, 19, 32 or 40	☐	☐
Comparison	If you agree to statements 10, 18, 38 or 48	☐	☐
Spirituality	If you agree to statements 3, 14, 35 or 46	☐	☐
Great Expectations	If you agree to statements 16, 27, 33 or 45	☐	☐
Conquest	If you agree to statements 7, 23, 41 or 44	☐	☐
Productivity	If you agree to statements 9, 17, 31 or 49	☐	☐
Criticism	If you agree to statements 12, 20 or 36	☐	☐

The CLS Survey covered a variety of thoughts, feelings, and actions. What is remarkable is that all of these seemingly different aspects of our lives are closely related. How this is possible becomes clearer when you understand more about CLS Addictions.

Conditional Love State (CLS) Addictions

The CLS Addictions are the ways we have been taught to seek love and acceptance. But, the tragedy is that their very nature actually prevents us from experiencing the love and acceptance we are looking for. We will now explore why these addictions can never be completely satisfied and how they impose limitations on our freedom.

Addictions – Yikes!

When we use the term addiction it is easy to make people feel uncomfortable and somewhat defensive. That is far from our intention. In fact, when we, the authors, began to examine our own personal addictions we found that we averaged 11 each. There is nothing to be ashamed about if you have a CLS Addiction. They are very real forces that can influence our lives in various ways. Identifying your addictions will help you better understand yourself and empower you to make changes at the deepest level.

How A CLS Addiction Works

To better understand how the CLS leads to addictive behavior we will be introducing the four components of an addiction. Since these addictions present an entirely new way of examining your life, new terms have been invented. Don't let this terminology intimidate you as the concepts are both simple to understand and easy to apply.

1) **CCLB - Central Conditional Love Belief:**

    The central belief of "I am not worthy of love and acceptance as I am" is the starting point of all CLS Addictions.

2) **CLR - Conditional Love Response:**

When we believe that we are not worthy of love and acceptance as we are (CCLB), we *respond* by searching for ways to prove ourselves more worthy of love. As a result, we have developed ideas of how we can prove our worthiness of love. Each idea is called a Conditional Love Response (CLR) and it determines the type of addiction we have.

3) **CLN - Conditional Love Need:**

These needs arise from our CLRs. They represent what we need in our lives to feel the love and acceptance we seek.

4) **CLA - Conditional Love Action:**

These actions arise from our CLNs. They are what we must do to satisfy our needs.

The Four Components of an Addiction

Central Conditional Love Belief (CCLB) → Conditional Love Response (CLR) → Conditional Love Need (CLN) → Conditional Love Action (CLA)

These terms will become clearer to you after you look at a few examples. As in all examples of this book, the names used have been altered to protect people's privacy.

Example 1 - Rachel's Climb Up the Corporate Ladder

Rachel is an executive in her early forties. Having a successful career is important to her self-worth. A senior position opens up in Rachel's firm that she has had her eyes on for years. To get the promotion, she works harder and puts in longer hours. Rachel is willing to sacrifice whatever she can to get the promotion because not getting it will make her feel like a failure. Let us look at how Rachel was able to break down her addiction.

Central Conditional Love Belief (CCLB):	→	Conditional Love Response (CLR):	→	Conditional Love Need (CLN):	→	Conditional Love Action (CLA):
I am not worthy of love and acceptance as I am.		I believe that I am more worthy of love and acceptance when I am successful.		I need to get the job promotion.		I will work harder. I will work longer hours. I will sacrifice time with my family to get this promotion.

In the above example, Rachel does not believe that she is acceptable unless she proves it (CCLB). Like many people, she believes that she must be successful to prove she is more worthy of acceptance (CLR). In order to meet her definition of success one of her needs is to be promoted (CLN). To fulfill this need Rachel works harder and puts in overtime (CLA). She has what is called a Success addiction because she needs to succeed in order to feel acceptable. Working towards a promotion is not what makes Rachel addicted. But, basing her worthiness of love and acceptance on getting the promotion does.

Example 2 - Vinay's Quest for Attention

Vinay is a man in his late twenties who is so handsome that he makes many women turn their heads. He has worked hard to build a muscular body and has noticed that this wins him even more attention. Every time a woman looks at Vinay with desire, he feels better about himself. On the other hand, when women are not attracted to him, he tends to feel somewhat insecure about his appearance. Whenever he fails to gain their attention, Vinay feels less acceptable as a person. Though Vinay may not be aware of all this on a conscious level, he works out regularly to fulfill his need for attention. Here is how Vinay broke down his addiction:

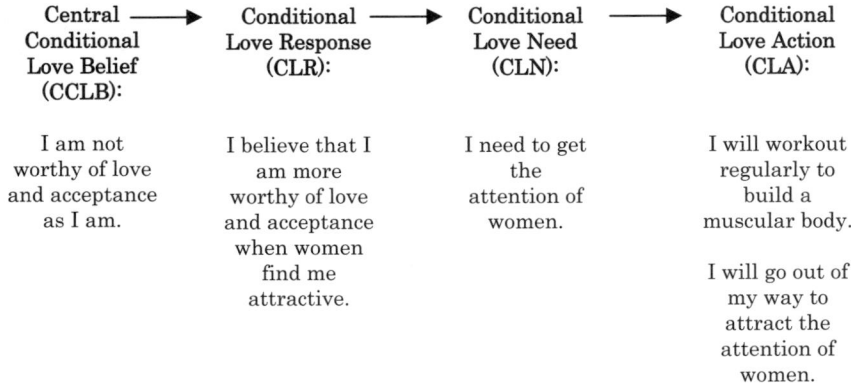

In this example, Vinay has a central belief that he needs to prove his worth before he can accept himself (CCLB). He believes that he can prove himself worthy of love when other women find him attractive (CLR). This belief creates the need to gain the attention of women (CLN). To fulfill this need, Vinay works out regularly (CLA). We can conclude that Vinay has what is called an Appearance addiction because Vinay is emotionally dependent on the attention he receives from other women.

It is important to stress that it is not the actions (CLAs) that make a person addicted. Striving for a promotion or a great body is not what led to Rachel and Vinay's respective addictions. It is the fact that they have associated their self-worth with being successful or getting attention. This is what makes them addicted. Consequently, they may feel that their self-acceptance is at stake whenever an opportunity for success or attention arises. Since feeling acceptable is one of our deepest needs, they are driven to continually strive for success or attention.

CLS Addictions are rooted in the belief that we must prove our worthiness of love and acceptance. As long as this belief prevails, we will feel compelled to validate our worth by meeting whatever conditions we have placed on our self-acceptance (e.g. success and attention as in the above examples).

CLS Addictions
A Breakthrough In Self-Awareness

Human behavior can be very complex. The great thing about breaking down CLS Addictions into their respective components is that it helps deepen our understanding of our behavior without simplifying things. Later you will have an opportunity to learn how to break down your own addictions. When you do, you will be amazed to see how insightful this process is. By determining the beliefs, needs and actions that make up your behavior, you will uncover many things that you never knew about yourself.

But, Are These Really Addictions?

We have described the behaviors in the CLS as addictions, but why have we chosen this seemingly extreme term? Quite simply, that is exactly what they are. To further appreciate why the term addiction is appropriate, let us now examine some of the similarities between CLS Addictions and substance addictions.

The withdrawal symptoms you can experience:

When substance addicts do not satisfy their addictions for some time, they experience withdrawal symptoms. The exact nature of these symptoms varies depending on the drug one is addicted to. Most often the withdrawal results in symptoms that are opposite in nature to the effects the drug produces. For example, cocaine addicts will experience emotional depression and fatigue as a consequence of withdrawal. These symptoms completely contrast with the elation that cocaine causes. As a result, the addict needs the cocaine to escape from the discomfort of the withdrawal symptoms.

Similarly, when you are unable to satisfy your CLS Addictions, you will experience the discomfort of feeling less worthy of acceptance. Though these withdrawal symptoms may not be physically apparent, they manifest emotionally as the stress, fear, or insecurity you experience when you are unable to prove your worth. These withdrawal symptoms differ entirely from the acceptance and contentment you feel when you fulfill your addictions. For example, having been unable to achieve anything of significance for some time, Success addicts will judge themselves to be less worthy of love and lose some of their self-confidence. To escape this sense of inadequacy, Success addicts will feel a strong need to reestablish their sense of acceptability by being successful.

The euphoria that keeps you wanting more:

The intense pleasure experienced from a drug is what gives an addict a sense of euphoria, otherwise known as a *fix*. The euphoria caused by the drug entices substance addicts to keep coming back for more. This helps to explain, in part, the self-perpetuating nature of an addiction. CLS Addictions are no different in this respect. Once you experience the relief of feeling worthy of acceptance, you will be motivated to keep doing whatever it takes to continue feeling that way.

In the CLS, you get your fix through proving your worthiness of love. Just as alcoholics are addicted to alcohol, when you are in the CLS you are addicted to what makes you feel more acceptable. You become addicted to these things because they give you a feeling of acceptance and love. But, as you will soon see, the feeling is short-lived, and it is not long before you are looking for your next fix. For example, despite the satisfaction Rachel and Vinay may experience from their addictions, it will not be long before they are trying to prove their worth once again. In this way, your need for self-acceptance can never be fulfilled through CLS Addictions. They only keep you needing more and more.

Addictions compensate for a deeper emotional need:

Substance addicts often start using drugs as a means of compensating for a deeper need. In many cases the drug is used as a form of escape, a way of covering up an emotional wound or filling an emptiness within.

CLS addicts seek to satisfy their addictions out of a deeper need as well, the need for complete love and acceptance from none other than themselves. For example, when Success addicts chase after success, it is not the success that they want, but what success has come to represent. When Appearance addicts chase after being beautiful, it is not the beauty that they want, but what the beauty allows them to feel. By achieving these things they allow themselves to feel the love and acceptance they long for. As you study how these addictions affect your life, you will understand how the central belief of the CLS prevents you from ever fulfilling your deeper need.

How Addictions Can Limit Your Freedom

Since Born on the Mountaintop deals with reclaiming your personal freedom, it is important to be clear about the influence addictions have on your freedom. Each CLS Addiction can limit your freedom on both emotional and physical levels. To fully appreciate this, in the sections to come you need to engage in an in-depth examination of your possible addictions. For example, to understand how your addictions may be limiting your emotional freedom, you can explore how they affect your ability to feel good about yourself right now. Do your addictions cause you to judge yourself in any way? When you cannot fulfill an addiction, does it lead to stress, fear, or insecurity? If so, how do you respond to these feelings?

Once you have assessed the emotional impact of your addictions, examine how they might be affecting your physical freedom by preventing you from living your life the way you want to. Do your addictions take time away from other things you would rather be doing? Do your addictions inhibit you from achieving or exploring what you really want from life?

By exploring the influence of each addiction on these aspects of your freedom, you will come to truly appreciate how the CLS is harming the quality of your life.

Taking An Honest Look:

In the following section, we will be describing the addictions in detail. At times, we will be pointing out how these addictions may be limiting your personal freedom. This does not mean that any of the addictions are good or bad. In fact, you may even notice that there are benefits to staying addicted, and that is perfectly alright. Keep in mind that the purpose of these descriptions is to become aware of how your addictions may be affecting you. This entails honestly looking at the disadvantages as well as the advantages of each.

As you read on, you will notice that many pages have been dedicated to helping you understand your addictions before even mentioning a possible alternative. This can be very frustrating for those anxious to find a quick fix. But we must stress again that this process of thoroughly understanding the CLS is absolutely necessary, because understanding a problem in its entirety is the key to solving it. In fact, making the mistake of rushing to solutions is one of the reasons the CLS and these addictions have eluded most people for so long. So tread slowly, as you take an honest look at yourself and how you interact with the world around you.

CONFIRMING WHICH ADDICTIONS YOU HAVE

We will now explore the twelve major CLS Addictions. After reflecting on the addictions, you will be able to confirm which of them are influencing your life.

> **If you can relate to some of the problems that arise in an addiction or find that it limits your freedom in any way, simply check the corresponding box under the *My Confirmed Addictions* column on page 51.**

Everyone is unique and will have their own set of addictions based on their life experiences. As you identify which addictions relate to you, consider how possible environmental influences may have created or reinforced your addictions. You may uncover that many of the addictions you have are interrelated, and that some are more dominant than others.

To further investigate each addiction, questions for reflection are provided. We recommend you take the time to answer them as this will help you determine how each addiction is affecting you.

THE ACCEPTANCE OF OTHERS ADDICTION

Can other people's opinions affect how you feel about yourself or the decisions you make? Have you ever wondered why it is so difficult to stop worrying about what other people think of you? When you believe that you are not worthy of love as you are, one of the common ways of trying to prove that you are worthy is through getting the acceptance of other people.

You have the Acceptance of Others addiction when one of your conditions for accepting yourself is having the approval of others.

The Acceptance of Others addiction is an excellent place to start our investigation of addictions because most of us are brought up to believe that we are more acceptable when other people accept us.

Some people with this addiction might seek the acceptance of only one person, while others may require the approval of almost every person they meet. Although there is nothing wrong with pleasing others, when you base your worthiness of love on their approval, it can severely inhibit your freedom.

When you have the Acceptance of Others addiction, you tend to look at yourself through the eyes of the people whose acceptance you desire. Since you cannot accept yourself if they reject you, their opinion of you becomes very important. Naturally, you cannot help but feel self-conscious around these people because only when they approve of you can you feel the self-love you need.

The Masks We Wear

In a way, this addiction prevents you from being yourself around the people whose acceptance you seek and forces you to wear masks. Instead of saying or doing what feels natural, you will find yourself conforming to what is expected of you. Even when these people are not around, their presence can be felt. In fact, any step outside the confines of what is considered acceptable by them can be difficult for you to take. Naturally, these restrictions may limit your options in life.

By masking your true self, the Acceptance of Others addiction prevents your unique personality from interacting with the world around you. This is a major loss because without honest self-expression, you can never know for sure who you really are. Nor can you experience the freedom of being yourself and watching your deepest wishes unfold. In this sense, the masks you wear not only hide you from other people, but they also hide you from yourself. Each time you forgo your deeper inclinations for what is expected of you, your energy goes into maintaining the image depicted by the mask rather than exploring who you really are.

The relationships that develop from the Acceptance of Others addiction are also affected by the masks worn. The masks you wear do not allow people to see you for who you truly are. The idiosyncrasies, thoughts and feelings that make up your unique personality remain hidden from view. Whenever you are afraid to share these parts of yourself, the relationships you develop become based more on an image than on a reality. Yet, deep relationships can only be experienced when you find the courage to remove your masks.

Although by removing your masks you may risk losing the acceptance of some people, the connections you do form will be stronger and more authentic. But, if you have the Acceptance of Others addiction it is hard to make these connections, because you cannot risk losing people's acceptance. If they do not accept you, you cannot accept yourself. Too much is at stake. Of course, you are not to blame for this. The nature of this addiction makes the wearing of masks necessary. As long as you believe that you must prove your self-worth, no matter how hard you try to stop worrying about what people think of you, you will never be able to. If you are looking for the courage to be yourself and to enjoy the benefits of living without masks, you must challenge the deep-rooted belief that you are not worthy of love as you are. It is this belief that creates the need for the acceptance of others in the first place.

An Example of the Acceptance of Others Addiction:

For as long as Curtis can remember he has loved composing and playing music on the piano. Few feelings can compare with the elation he experiences as his hands float across the keys. After years of hard work and dedication, Curtis has now become an accomplished pianist and wants to pursue a career as a musician. However, his parents have always believed it would be more practical for him to become a lawyer, and during heated discussions they expressed their disapproval for his musical aspirations.

Throughout his life, Curtis always depended on the emotional support of his parents. Knowing they were against him was something he found too difficult to bear. To avoid losing their acceptance he gave up his passion for music to pursue a career in law.

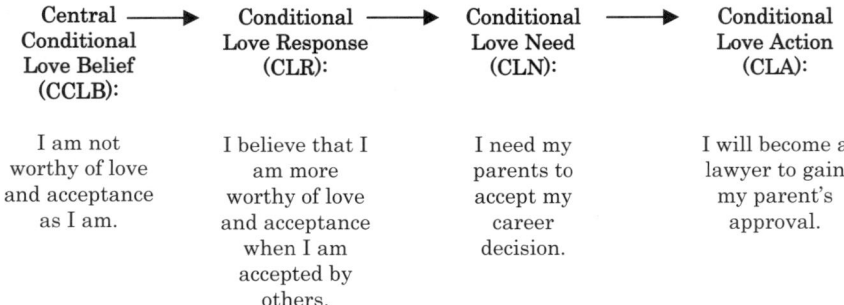

Central Conditional Love Belief (CCLB):	Conditional Love Response (CLR):	Conditional Love Need (CLN):	Conditional Love Action (CLA):
I am not worthy of love and acceptance as I am.	I believe that I am more worthy of love and acceptance when I am accepted by others.	I need my parents to accept my career decision.	I will become a lawyer to gain my parent's approval.

In this example, Curtis decides to become a lawyer out of a need to please his parents. His decision to become a lawyer is not what makes Curtis addicted. What makes him addicted is his belief that he is not worthy of love without the approval of his parents. Due to this belief Curtis **needs** his parents to approve of his career decision, even if it means sacrificing what is important to him. Unfortunately, his sacrifices will not end here. He will likely feel the need to give up many things in the future to keep satisfying this addiction.

Questions for Reflection:

1) Are there people whose acceptance or approval you would like to have? If so, who are they?

2) How would you feel if you did not gain the acceptance of these people?

3) Is there anything you are doing to gain the acceptance of these people?

4) Are you preventing yourself from doing anything in order to keep their acceptance?

If you can relate to some of the problems that arise in this addiction or find that it limits your freedom in any way, simply check the *My Confirmed Addictions* box for the Acceptance of Others addiction on page 51.

THE JUGGLING ACT

When you have the Acceptance of Others addiction, trying to meet people's expectations can be a juggling act. This is because most people you encounter have their own conditions that you need to fulfill before they will accept you. As a result, you will have to fulfill each of their conditions in order to feel good about yourself. Even if there are only a handful of people whose acceptance you seek, juggling all these conditions can be a very demanding process. Just drop one "ball," and watch how your self-worth begins to fall with it.

THE PERFECTION ADDICTION

Do you get frustrated with yourself when you make a mistake or when things are not going perfectly? Does the need for perfection affect your freedom to enjoy your life and be at peace? If so, we will get to the bottom of what is happening with this next CLS Addiction.

When you are in the CLS, another way you may try to prove that you are worthy of love is by being perfect in certain areas of your life. Wanting to improve yourself can be a noble intention. Striving for perfection can push you to learn more and do things you never thought possible. Yet, anyone with the Perfection addiction will admit that this desire to improve can get out-of-hand. Your troubles begin once believe that you have to prove your worthiness of love and acceptance.

> **You have the Perfection addiction if you believe that you must meet your ideals of perfection before you can feel completely acceptable.**

Do not be dissuaded by the word perfect. Even if you have the need to be near perfect before you can accept yourself, you likely have this addiction.

An Example of the Perfection Addiction:

Jennifer is an example of a caring woman who believes that her worthiness of acceptance is based on being an ideal mother and wife. Whenever there is tension in the family, she tends to assume responsibility for it. Even when she has less control over a situation, like an argument between her husband and daughter, she will still drain her energy trying to maintain peace within the family. This often occurs at the expense of the things she wants to do and, sometimes, even at the expense of her health. Here is how Jennifer breaks down her addiction:

Central Conditional Love Belief (CCLB):	→ Conditional Love Response (CLR):	→ Conditional Love Need (CLN):	→ Conditional Love Action (CLA):
I am not worthy of love and acceptance as I am.	I believe that I am more worthy of love and acceptance when I am perfect."	I need to be an ideal mother and wife	I will try to mitigate any tension that arises in the family.

Wanting to be an ideal mother and wife can be a meaningful goal. However when Jennifer started to base her self-worth on reaching this goal, she began to lose her freedom to feel good about herself. Now, as long as there is peace in the family she is able to feel acceptable. But, if anything goes wrong, even things outside her control, Jennifer will be hard on herself. Anything that threatens her status as a perfect mom or wife will deprive her of the self-love she emotionally depends on.

Perfection and Your Emotional Freedom

The need for perfection can take a tremendous toll on your emotional well-being. To hold yourself accountable to such high standards is not easy, especially when you base your self-acceptance on meeting them. Whenever you fail to meet any of your ideals, you will automatically judge yourself to be less worthy of love. This self-judgment does not help you improve, but actually drains the very energy you could put towards improving the situation. Also if you ever manage to achieve perfection in anything, your self-acceptance will be vulnerable to anything that challenges what you have achieved.

As in the case of Jennifer, you may even become threatened by things outside your control. It is difficult to find peace of mind without acknowledging that circumstances outside your control can prevent perfection from ever being reached. Consequently, the Perfection addiction prevents you from establishing a healthy relationship with the world around you. If you have the Perfection addiction, you may agree with this in theory, but deep down you will continue to be enslaved to your need for perfection.

After all, acceptance is one of your deepest emotional needs, and this addiction will only allow you to experience it when you reach your ideals of perfection. In all other circumstances, you are left feeling less worthy of love.

Considering how emotionally demanding the Perfection addiction is, you would expect satisfying this addiction to be very rewarding. Unfortunately, this is not the case because there are an infinite number of ways to be imperfect, but only one way of being perfect. As a result, Perfection addicts must endure the stress and self-judgment that arises from the addiction with very few, if any, opportunities to feel completely good about themselves.

A Mistaken Perspective

If you have difficulty accepting mistakes, you likely have the Perfection addiction. After all, a mistake is a sign that you are not quite perfect. The fear of making mistakes not only leads to stress, but also prevents addicts from taking chances and trying to do the things they want. It is not surprising that many of us grow up condemning mistakes because we live in a culture that fails to acknowledge mistakes as part of the learning process. Instead, people are usually pitied for the mistakes they make. However, no one can possibly grow without making mistakes. The author Stephan Manes wisely observed, "Perfect is never doing anything wrong – which means never doing anything at all." Giving yourself room to make mistakes allows you to participate in the thrill of living life. By letting go of the need to be perfect you give yourself the freedom to learn from your experiences.

That being said, it is important to understand that you cannot let go of the need to be perfect without addressing the real problem – the belief that you are not worthy of love as you are. The addiction and its limitations on your freedom exist because you are trying to avoid the painful possibility of feeling unworthy of love. Such a possibility is only present because you have been convinced that you must prove you are worthy of love and acceptance. By breaking free from this belief, you can work towards improving yourself in whatever way you want, without experiencing the limitations of the Perfection addiction.

Questions for Reflection:

1) What are some areas in your life that you are trying to improve upon? (Consider work, family life, hobbies, social interactions, your thoughts, feelings, etc.)

2) Do you experience any pressure to be perfect in any of these areas of your life? If so, how does this pressure affect you?

3) Recall when you made a mistake in any of the above areas of your life. How did this make you feel?

4) Are there any challenges that you are avoiding? Explore how this could be related to the fear of making mistakes.

If you can relate to some of the problems that arise in this addiction or find that it limits your freedom in any way, simply check the *My Confirmed Addictions* box for the Perfection addiction on page 51.

Satyam's Corner
NEVER LET THEM SEE YOU SWEAT

I have realized, through my own experience, that the desire to control our emotions is a classic symptom of the Perfection addiction. When I was a boy, I was taught that anger is not a "positive" emotion and I should be in control of it. Due to this experience and my need to be as close to perfect as possible, I began to believe that I was less worthy of love if I lost my composure. Consequently, whenever I felt angry, I tried to control the feeling or suppress it. Later, I learned that most people are brought up to cope with their anger in the same way.

Anger is not the only emotion that many of us are taught to suppress. In some environments, showing uncertainty is a sign of weakness. For example, in the corporate world, the pressure of having to conceal any insecurity or confusion can lead to a great deal of internalized stress. It is amazing how many rash decisions are made in the boardroom just because people are afraid to admit their uncertainty. People are also raised to believe that crying is a sign of weakness. As a physical therapist, I have often consoled mourning family members who apologized for their tears. They were convinced that they should be "stronger." In the name of being "strong" they felt pressured to suppress the very emotions that make them human.

Although I am not in favor of taking our anger out on others or becoming crippled by our emotions, I do believe that suppressing our feelings has serious consequences on our health. Instead of denying the sadness, anger, uncertainty, or fear that we experience, we must first learn to acknowledge and accept them. Only through completely accepting how we feel can we understand our emotions and effectively work on improving these aspects of our lives. However, this poses a dilemma for Perfection addicts. How can they develop a healthy approach to their emotions when they believe certain emotions make them less worthy of love? Quite simply, they cannot. That is why most people with the Perfection addiction are compelled to suppress some of their feelings rather than acknowledge them. Unfortunately, when emotions are denied like this they are left to resurface later, often in the form of mental or physical ailments.

The Appearance Addiction

Do you ever feel self-conscious about your appearance? Do you feel the pressure to live up to any standards of beauty? In a world where we are constantly being bombarded with glamorized images of beautiful people, another way that we may try to prove that we are worthy of love is by seeking to be attractive.

You have the Appearance addiction when you believe that you need to be physically attractive before you can feel completely acceptable.

Understanding the Appearance addiction will help you appreciate how your freedom can be inhibited when you base your self-acceptance on your body image.

The Fix from Looking Good

If you have the Appearance addiction, you may be self-conscious about your looks. In order to get your *fix* from this addiction you will seek attention from other people as a means of validating your acceptability. When people notice you, you will feel better about yourself, and your confidence will grow. On the other hand, when you do not get this attention you may feel insecure. By basing your self-worth on your appearance, you leave your emotional well-being at the mercy of how others perceive you.

Even if you are considered attractive by many people, the Appearance addiction can still affect how you feel. This happens when being attractive becomes one of your sources of self-acceptance – a foundation of your self-esteem. If people do not find you attractive, you will end up questioning your acceptability. This is why it is common for attractive people to feel pressured to maintain their appearance. They cannot afford to lose their fix of acceptance.

Old age is something Appearance addicts can have difficulty dealing with. They can struggle against the changes their bodies go through because they cannot emotionally afford to lose the youthful appearance that is a source of their self-worth. In their eyes, the natural process of growing older has become equivalent to no longer being acceptable.

The Psychological Damage

There is nothing wrong with wanting to look attractive. No one can deny that being attractive has its benefits. However, the idea that being attractive is needed to prove that one is worthy of love is responsible for much of the self-judgment people inflict on themselves.

When you have the Appearance addiction and identify flaws in your appearance, you can be especially hard on yourself. The nagging feeling that "my thighs are too big," or "my biceps are too small" can inhibit you from ever feeling completely acceptable. In addition, you may experience the discomfort that comes from comparing how you look to others. When you encounter people who you perceive to be more attractive than you are, you cannot help but feel somewhat inadequate.

By treating yourself this way, you are essentially telling yourself that you are unworthy of love until you look the way you think you should. This is a very painful message. Just imagine if someone who professed to love you said that he or she could not accept you until you changed the way you looked. Most people would question the sincerity of that kind of love. Yet, is this not the same message you are giving yourself every time you base your self-acceptance on looking a certain way? The pressure that arises from the Appearance addiction may motivate you to make healthy lifestyle changes such as changing your diet or exercising. But, when these changes are made to prove your worthiness of love, the psychological damage will outweigh the possible benefits.

Here is an example of how the Appearance addiction may affect someone in the CLS:

Central Conditional Love Belief (CCLB):	Conditional Love Response (CLR):	Conditional Love Need (CLN):	Conditional Love Action (CLA):
I am not worthy of love and acceptance as I am.	I believe that I am more worthy of love and acceptance when I look beautiful.	I need to lose weight and get in shape. I need people to be attracted to me.	I will go on a diet. I will workout at the gym every day. I will try to get the attention of others and judge myself if I cannot.

Ultimately, it is the belief that we are not worthy of love as we are that is behind the Appearance addiction. Due to this belief, we forsake our ability to accept ourselves as we are and engage in an unnecessary struggle for attention through trying to look a certain way.

Fortunately, we will explore a way to break free from addictions. In a later chapter, you will be empowered with a way of perceiving yourself that will give you the freedom to feel good about yourself regardless of how you look.

Questions for Reflection:

1) Do you have an idea of how your body should look? If so, how do you feel when you do not look the way you want?

2) How do you feel when other people are attracted to you because of your appearance? Do you feel differently when people do not notice you?

3) Is there anything you are doing to draw people's attention to how you look?

4) Do you avoid certain situations because of how you look?

If you can relate to some of the problems that arise in this addiction or find that it limits your freedom in any way, simply check the *My Confirmed Addictions* box for the Appearance addiction on page 51.

Who Defines What is Beautiful?

We all have ideas of what is beautiful and what is not. Where do these ideas come from? Most often the body images that we compare ourselves to have been defined by the media. Multi-billion dollar industries, such as the cosmetics and fashion industries, use television and magazine advertisements to convince us that buying certain products will help us become beautiful. Each of their ads portray images of "beautiful" people who seem confident and secure about themselves. Subconsciously we begin to believe that if we looked like these people, we could feel better about ourselves too. Once we believe this, we become imprisoned to an often-unattainable standard of "beauty." But, what gives these companies the right to define how we should look? Who gives them the authority to dictate any ideal of beauty? We do, and unless we reclaim our right to feel good about ourselves no matter how we look, we cannot be free.

The Success Addiction

Success can be defined in many ways. Some of us might equate success to money or to the love of our family and friends, while others may define success by their personal achievements in life.

How would you feel if you did not achieve the success you desire? Most people confess that they would feel disappointed in themselves. If you feel the same, where does your disappointment come from? Do you know why you give such importance to achieving success?

Often we tend to value success because our society glorifies triumph. We are taught at a very young age that the successful deserve praise and are more worthy of love. We are conditioned to believe that only the winners have cause to celebrate while the losers have cause to mourn their shortcomings. Since most of us are in the CLS and are struggling to validate our self-worth, it is not surprising that many of us aspire for success.

You have the Success addiction when you believe that being successful or achieving something is necessary before you can feel completely acceptable.

The desire to grow and progress through success can be healthy, but when it is motivated by a need for acceptance it will plunge you into an endless pursuit of measuring yourself against the quality of your achievements.

Overlooking the Process

If you have the Success addiction you will not let yourself feel worthy of acceptance until you succeed. In the meantime, most of your time will be spent stressfully pursuing your goals. Although the stress can motivate you, it also makes it difficult for you to enjoy the process. In a culture where success is emphasized so much, this process is often overlooked. It seems that we take for granted that success will make us happy. However, whenever our need for success comes from an addiction it will fail to deliver this happiness. Although we may enjoy temporary satisfaction we will soon need to achieve more success to feel better about ourselves. This makes it especially important to consider the journey towards success. After all, the glory of success only lasts for a short time, while the process of achieving a goal is what makes up the majority of our life experience. By missing out on the process, we can end up missing our lives.

The Success Addiction can Actually Prevent Us from Being Successful

For Success addicts failure is proof of not being worthy of the love and acceptance they long for. That is why the Success addiction can burden you with the fear of failure while trying to achieve your goals. Even when you are successful, you can experience a fear of losing the success you have achieved. Such a turn of events would deprive you of your source of acceptability.

If you have the Success addiction, no matter how successful you may be, the fear of failure is one of the biggest obstacles to realizing your full potential. It blocks the flow of creative thought and drains your energy. The fear of failure can also prevent you from taking needed risks. Those afflicted by this fear may not realize that all worthwhile achievements are attained by enduring some failures along the way. In fact, failures are powerful mentors. They leave precious clues to success. When you view failure as an integral part of the learning process, you are less likely to take it personally and more likely to evolve at a faster pace. Naturally, businesses that adopt fear-based cultures struggle with maintaining high levels of positive energy among members of their work force.

If too much importance is given to achieving a goal, you run the risk of rushing through things. Too many people make this mistake. It is easy to become so fixated on reaching a destination that you do not plan and execute to the best of your abilities. Ironically, the need to succeed prevents you from being as successful as you could be if your self-esteem was not attached to the outcome.

An Example of the Success addiction:

Throughout the years, Andrew has taken great pride in being a successful real estate agent. As a result, he bases a lot of his self-worth on how successful he is. This year, his goal is to be the number one salesperson in his region. To do this, he plans to sell one house every week. Whenever he achieves this goal he feels great about himself, and whenever he does not he feels unhappy.

During the year, Andrew harbors a fear of failing to achieve his goal because being a successful real estate agent has become a vital source of his self-esteem. The fear of not succeeding has started making him nervous during sales calls and presentations. This bothers Andrew because he knows that this fear is inhibiting his performance. He has lost the liberty to be as comfortable as he would like, and this prevents him from making the most out of his interactions with prospects.

Central Conditional Love Belief (CCLB):	→ Conditional Love Response (CLR):	→ Conditional Love Need (CLN):	→ Conditional Love Action (CLA):
I am not worthy of love and acceptance as I am.	I believe that I am more worthy of love and acceptance when I am a success.	I need to be the number one real estate agent in my region.	I will try to sell one house every week and feel bad whenever I fail.

The Success addiction is driven by the belief that we must prove our worthiness of love and acceptance. Andrew's problem is not that he wants to be successful. The CCLB makes proving his worth an absolute necessity, and success is Andrew's way of doing this. If Andrew can break free from his Success addiction at the level of this central belief, he will have the freedom to apply his full potential towards whatever success he wants and still feel good about himself along the way.

Questions for Reflection:

1) How do you define success for yourself?

2) How would you feel if you failed to achieve the success you desire?

3) What are you doing to achieve success? Is there anything of importance to you that you are sacrificing or neglecting in order to succeed?

If you can relate to some of the problems that arise in this addiction or find that it limits your freedom in any way, simply check the *My Confirmed Addictions* box for the Success addiction on page 51.

"THE ONE" ADDICTION

Do you feel pressured to find that special someone to share your life with? If you are in a relationship, can you be completely honest with your partner? Relationships can be fantastic experiences. Each person we share emotional or physical intimacy with can be a source of growth, support, and joy. However, when we have "The One" addiction, our perspective on relationships can prevent us from experiencing the benefits of being with someone we love.

> **You have "The One" addiction when you base some of your self-worth on being in an intimate relationship or finding that one special person to share your life with.**

It is not difficult to discover where this addiction comes from. Popular movies, television shows, and music often describe people struggling to find the love they long for in the arms of another.

> "I think he is the one!" she whispers to her friends at the café. She never looked happier.

> "She is the one for me, and I can't bear the thought of living without her," he declared before storming out of the room.

> "I don't want to lose him. What if he is the one?" she says as she contemplates the possibility of living the rest of her life alone.

These are just a few examples of the way this addiction is projected from the silver screen into our minds. When you combine this with the fact that many people pity those who reach a certain age without finding a life-partner, it is hard not to feel disappointed with being single. The notion that there is something wrong with being alone is so prevalent that many of us believe that we are not acceptable unless we are in a relationship.

With all the pressure to be with someone, many of us never question whether a relationship is something we even want. When we are alone, instead of enjoying our solitude we end up feeling that we are inadequate or that there is something deeply missing in our lives. In some cases, this pressure to be with "the one" can make couples feel that they must marry each other prematurely or continue to stay in relationships that are clearly not healthy.

"The One" Addiction Creates Fantasy Relationships

Most people with "The One" addiction have some idea of the type of person they are looking for. That is why most relationships begin with both partners having definite expectations of each other. As long as the couple continues to live up to each other's expectations, the relationship has a chance of surviving. Since both people in the relationship know this, the fear of losing "the one" pressures them into meeting those expectations. For example, it may lead to subtle changes in their behavior such as holding back their true feelings or not sharing parts of their personalities. By placing these expectations on each other in a relationship, the couple unintentionally restricts each other's personal development within the expectations they have of "the one." Whenever someone does not fit the ideal of "the one," love is withdrawn from him or her.

Although the tendency to withdraw love when our partner does not meet our expectations is common, this arrangement seems more like a contract than love. In such relationships, both parties trade in their freedom and agree to live within the boundaries of each other's fantasies. If they can continue to be "the one" of each other's dreams, they will enjoy each other's love. Yet, the moment one of them fails to live up to these expectations the contract will be breached, and the relationship will be threatened.

An Example of "The One" Addiction:

Ronald has been looking to find a woman with whom he can share his life with for years. One day, his friends introduced him to a woman named Angela. After a couple of dates, Ronald knew he liked her. He felt a chemistry between them that was unlike anything he had ever experienced before. She is smart, funny, charming, and successful; everything he hoped for in a woman. When they first began seeing each other, Ronald hesitated to invest too much emotion in the relationship because he was afraid of getting hurt. At the same time, he liked her and tried his best to keep her interested in him. As he became more comfortable in the relationship, he was more open with his feelings.

Ronald felt like Angela filled a big gap in his life, and he felt great knowing that his quest to find "the one" was finally over. Everything was going well until Angela broke up with him because she no longer felt that they were compatible. Ronald was crushed by the breakup. Months later, Ronald was still having trouble picking up the pieces of his life. This was partly because he missed her, but mostly because he believed that he needed to be in a relationship before he could feel good about himself again.

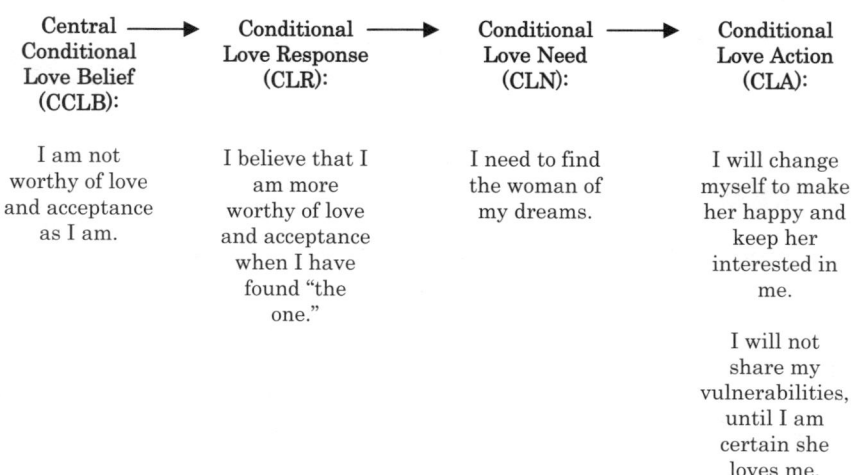

Central Conditional Love Belief (CCLB):	Conditional Love Response (CLR):	Conditional Love Need (CLN):	Conditional Love Action (CLA):
I am not worthy of love and acceptance as I am.	I believe that I am more worthy of love and acceptance when I have found "the one."	I need to find the woman of my dreams.	I will change myself to make her happy and keep her interested in me. I will not share my vulnerabilities, until I am certain she loves me.

When Ronald first began to see Angela, he did not want to feel vulnerable. He knew that if he invested too much of himself in the relationship, he would risk getting hurt if she did not reciprocate his feelings. This is a common approach to relationships and raises an important question:

Why do we get hurt when people we love do not love us in return?

By taking a closer look at "The One" addiction, the answer to this question is revealed. If you have "The One" addiction, you believe finding that special person who loves you is necessary to feel acceptable. This means that when you fall in love with someone, the way he or she feels about you helps determine how you feel about yourself. In this way, rejection is no longer just a question of incompatibility. It becomes a real threat to your self-esteem.

On the other hand, whenever someone reciprocates your love, you feel like a gap in your life has been filled. However, what you have actually filled is the condition placed on your ability to accept yourself. "The One" addiction makes you feel that you need the love of another, when what you are really looking for is the love of yourself. If you have this addiction, you have been brought up to believe that you can only give yourself this love when you find "the one." As with all addictions, satisfying "The One" addiction can only give you temporary fulfillment. The underlying belief that you are not worthy of love as you are must be challenged if you want to fill the real gap in your life. Until then you will always be looking for one way or another to prove that you are acceptable.

This does not belittle the chemistry and good times Ronald and Angela may have shared. As social beings, we share a wonderful opportunity to relate and connect with one another. Yet, the need to find or keep "the one" will always limit the freedom to build healthy relationships. When you have "The One" addiction, you believe that you are not worthy of love as you are. With this perspective, it is very difficult to love someone else when you have not found the strength to love yourself. When you break free from "The One" addiction, you can experience relationships that are free from the fear of losing the other person and do not require meeting each other's expectations.

Questions for Reflection:

1) Do you feel it is important to have a partner with whom to share your life? If so, why?

2 i) If you are not in a relationship, are you afraid of not finding someone to share your life with? If so, explore where this fear is coming from.

 ii) If you are in a relationship, how would you feel if your partner left you?

3) When you are in a relationship, do you change your behavior or hold parts of yourself back? If so, explore what is making you do this.

4) Do you have expectations of how "the one" should be in your life? If so, how do you think these expectations affect your partner?

If you can relate to some of the problems that arise in this addiction or find that it limits your freedom in any way, simply check the *My Confirmed Addictions* box for the "The One" addiction on page 51.

The Save The World Addiction

We are surrounded with news of corruption, crime, pollution, and violence. How do you feel when you hear about such problems in the world? Do you feel helpless or guilty for not doing your share to make a difference? Many individuals in the world are dedicating their lives to making positive changes. Unfortunately, some of these people experience emotional burnouts or breakdowns. Why does trying to make the world a better place become a draining experience for so many people? When you are in the CLS, even the positive intention of helping others can be motivated by the need to prove your worth. That is what makes this next addiction responsible for the feelings of guilt and frustration that people experience as they work towards helping others.

> **You have the Save the World addiction when you believe that you must make a positive impact on the world before you can feel completely acceptable.**

Trying to make the world a better place is an admirable cause. There is no doubt that the world could benefit from a lot more people trying to help others. If you start to believe that you cannot feel good about yourself until you make an impact on whatever social problems you are concerned with, you develop the Save the World addiction. When this happens, you actually end up limiting your capacity to make a difference.

Losing the Power to Make a Difference

When you have the Save the World addiction, your great intentions become undermined by your need to validate your worth. Though it may motivate you to help others, this addiction is a source of stress that can only limit your effectiveness and emotionally enslave you to your cause. What makes matters worse, most of the challenges Save the World addicts face are too complex for any one person to solve. Your need to prove your worth can compel you to assume responsibility for things outside of your control. Inevitably, this makes you lose perspective on what is actually in your control. The contributions you can make are compromised by worrying about things that are outside your realm of influence.

An Example of the Save the World Addiction:

Mary is a social worker who is committed to alleviating poverty in her community. She has spent the last nine years working for a non-profit organization that helps to empower the poor of her community. Mary has realized, to her dismay, that despite the positive influence of her work on some people's lives, poverty is increasing. She is terribly upset by the situation and feels inadequate for not doing enough. She is also depressed by her inability to make a sufficient impact on her community. It is clear that Mary is addicted to making a noticeable social difference. Since she has taken personal responsibility for finding a solution, she cannot accept herself until she does.

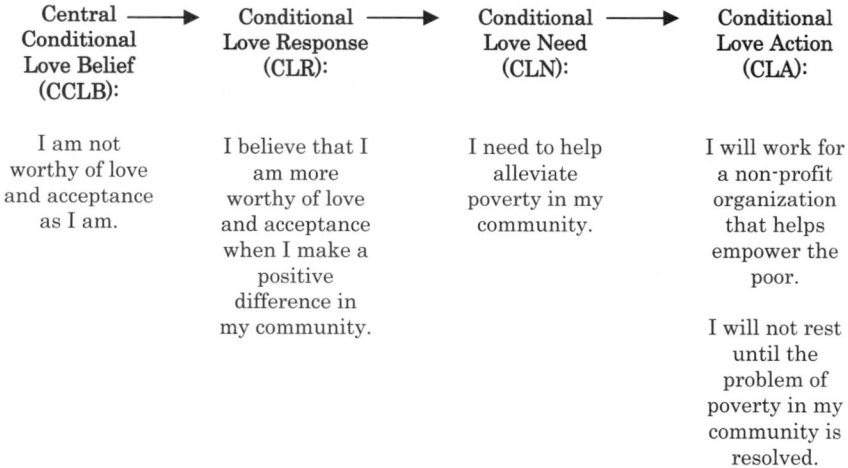

Central Conditional Love Belief (CCLB):	→	Conditional Love Response (CLR):	→	Conditional Love Need (CLN):	→	Conditional Love Action (CLA):
I am not worthy of love and acceptance as I am.		I believe that I am more worthy of love and acceptance when I make a positive difference in my community.		I need to help alleviate poverty in my community.		I will work for a non-profit organization that helps empower the poor. I will not rest until the problem of poverty in my community is resolved.

Mary's need to prove her worthiness of acceptance pushes her to make a positive change in her community. Though she is helping others, she is also hurting herself in the process. Her emotional dependence on the outcome of her work creates stress in her life that does more to hold her back than to help her cause. Her stress prevents her from addressing the problems of poverty with a fresh mind. Instead, she ends up being hard on herself and approaching challenges with the fear of not being able to do enough. In fact, basing her self-worth on the outcome of her work is resulting in an emotional burnout. Some people argue that without the pressure to prove her self-worth, Mary would become apathetic. This is unlikely. If Mary breaks free from the need to prove her worth, she will be empowered with the freedom to focus on what she can control, rather then worrying about the things she cannot. The mental energy that was lost banging her head in frustration can now be channeled towards coming up with more creative solutions to further her cause. More importantly, when she frees herself from this addiction she can enjoy her work, and that will give her more energy to help others.

Questions for Reflection:

1) How do you feel when you hear about all the problems in the world?

2) Do you feel that it is your responsibility to make a difference? How would you feel if you could not live up to this responsibility?

3) Do you feel a pressure to make a difference? If so, what are you doing?

If you can relate to some of the problems that arise in this addiction or find that it limits your freedom in any way, simply check the *My Confirmed Addictions* box for the Save the World addiction on page 51.

Freedom's Corner
WE ARE PART OF THE PROBLEM

When I was in university many years ago, I struggled a lot with the Save the World addiction. I was so dedicated to making a positive difference that I co-founded an organization called C.H.A.N.G.E. (Coalition for Humanitarian Action and New Global Empowerment). We started as a group of idealists sincerely dedicated to resolving some widespread global issues.

As we grew bigger, we began to experience conflict within the group that resulted in petty arguments and backbiting. We even had a few individuals who began to divide the group out of their own struggle for power. I was startled and disturbed by how the group began to manifest the very same conflicts we were trying to resolve. It became apparent that our need to change the world was not entirely coming from the selfless place that we had thought, but from a need to validate ourselves.

This was a painful realization for me. Not just due to all of the time and energy I invested in C.H.A.N.G.E. but more because I began to realize that my efforts were misdirected. I realized then that we could not make any lasting and meaningful changes in the world unless we first addressed the violence within our own thinking. Until then, the need to prove our worthiness of acceptance will get in the way of the cooperation required to tackle any of the local or global challenges we face.

For those of you who want to make a positive difference in the world, you will be amazed to realize how much of the global destruction is related to our need to fulfill CLS Addictions. As you read on, you will begin to understand how we cannot hope to heal the world until we each heal ourselves from the belief that we are not worthy of love as we are.

The Comparison Addiction

Think about a quality or talent you have that makes you feel good about yourself. If everyone else had that same quality or talent would you still feel good? Probably not. Often the things that give us pride come from comparing ourselves to others. Your investigation of the Comparison addiction will help you understand why this is the case. In particular, you will explore how the need to compare yourself with others can rob you of your ability to know yourself and live your life the way you want.

> **You have the Comparison Addiction when you base some of your worthiness of love on how well you compare to other people.**

One does not have to look far to uncover where this addiction comes from. Throughout our lives we have been compared to other people. As children, whenever we proved ourselves to be better than others, we were usually showered with praise and affection. Not surprisingly, many of us have grown up believing that we are not worthy of love unless we are doing well in comparison to others.

Losing Track of What Matters to You

Lisa is an example of a young woman with a Comparison addiction. Ever since she was young, Lisa's parents compared her to her older sister, Sarah. After years of receiving love based on how well she compared to Sarah, Lisa began to base her self-acceptance on outdoing her sister.

As an adult, some of Lisa's ambitions still come from a need to outdo Sarah. For example, just recently Lisa came to learn that Sarah bought a luxury car. Even though Lisa was content with her car, she began to feel envious because it was not as extravagant as her sister's car. In order to keep up with her sister, Lisa is now seriously considering saving enough money to buy a better car. Here is a breakdown of her addiction:

Central Conditional Love Belief (CCLB):	→ Conditional Love Response (CLR):	→ Conditional Love Need (CLN):	→ Conditional Love Action (CLA):
I am not worthy of love and acceptance as I am.	I believe that I am more worthy of love and acceptance when I am better than others.	I need to keep up with my sister and try to outdo her.	I will buy a better car than my sister's.

As soon as Lisa heard that Sarah had bought a luxury car, Lisa's self-acceptance was threatened. Since she could not afford to feel less accomplished than her older sister, she needed to buy a luxury car as well. Regardless of whether she had any genuine interest in buying this car, her Comparison addiction made it necessary for her to do so.

Notice how this addiction blinds Lisa into making important decisions based on what her sister does, rather than on what is important to her. This is a hallmark feature of the Comparison addiction. Those who have it tend to base their decisions on what other people are doing. Since there are so many ways that we can compare ourselves to others (including our job, assets, reputation, personality, looks, and even our front lawn), the need to fulfill the Comparison addiction can prevent us from uncovering what we really want from life. If we can remove these distractions, however, we can connect to our deeper drive in life, which is always more inspiring than the motivations we borrow from others.

The Monster of Jealousy

Whenever you are tempted to compare yourself with others, there is the possibility of encountering the *big green monster* of jealousy. If you have ever been jealous of someone, you can appreciate how horrible it feels. The emotion can eat you up inside and can result in malicious thoughts and actions. From childhood, we are all taught that jealousy is bad, but how can we avoid it when we are constantly being compared to others? More importantly, how can we avoid jealousy when we are led to believe that our worthiness of love is dependent on how we rank against others? Unless we break free from the Comparison addiction we will remain susceptible to this insecurity.

Unhealthy Competition

By competing with other people, you can push yourself to the next level and stretch your limits. The desire to improve yourself can result in healthy competition. However, the Comparison addiction occurs when you engage in the unhealthy practice of basing your self-acceptance on how well you rank against others. Competing with this mentality puts your self-esteem on the line. When you become emotionally dependent on being better than others, the outcome of any competition will define how you feel about yourself. When you win you will feel good, and when you lose you will feel awful. That is why the Comparison addiction makes people feel that nothing is as important as winning.

Not only can this addiction lead to a great deal of frustration, it can also inhibit your ability to compete. The fear of losing can cloud your mind and prevent you from taking your performance to the next level, whether it is a round of golf or a business you are running. Even when you do win, the confidence you gain with an addiction is fragile and will be shattered the next time you lose. Anything that challenges your victory will always have a power over you. Breaking free from the Comparison addiction will allow you to feel complete self-acceptance regardless of how you compare with others. Also, when you are less concerned about what the outcome will be, you can focus your entire energy on competing to the best of your ability.

Questions for Reflection:

1) Who are the people you compare yourself with? What aspects of your life do you compare?

2) When you realize someone is better than you at something you value, how does it make you feel?

3) Are you doing anything to prove that you are better than others? If so, what?

If you can relate to some of the problems that arise in this addiction or find that it limits your freedom in any way, simply check the *My Confirmed Addictions* box for the Comparison addiction on page 51.

"WHOEVER HAS THE MOST TOYS, WINS"

Comparing ourselves with other people begins at a very young age. If you visit any neighborhood playground, you will find children comparing their toys and clothes with each other. For children, keeping up with the latest trends is a serious matter. After all, the acceptance of their peers is at stake and this affects their ability to accept themselves.

For most people this does not change in adulthood. Instead of comparing little plastic toys, adults find themselves comparing much bigger "toys" like their cars, homes, jewelry and the latest gadgets. "Whoever has the most toys, wins" continues to be the principle by which people lead their lives. There is nothing wrong with this, so long as the "toys" you are seeking are what you truly want. However, if you are accumulating these "toys" just to prove your worth, you may end up sacrificing your freedom in exchange.

The Spirituality Addiction

Spirituality is a difficult word to define. For different people it can mean different things. Some people believe spirituality relates to an inner connection, others feel it is about how we treat our fellow brothers and sisters, and there are those who think that attaining an enlightened state of being is what makes someone more spiritual.

> **Regardless of what your definition of spirituality is, you have the Spirituality addiction if you feel less worthy of acceptance when you cannot live up to your spiritual ideals.**

The CLS reinforces a tendency to turn every endeavor into a way of validating our worth. Spiritual goals are not exceptions. If you feel stressed or guilty when you fail to live up to your spiritual ideals, the Spirituality addiction is the cause.

The Hierarchy of Spirituality

Just as people base their status on their financial net worth, there is a tendency among many of us to measure ourselves based on how far we have advanced along a "spiritual journey" Hierarchies have emerged in different spiritual communities, each with its own steps to the ultimate states of higher consciousness and peace. In these spiritual circles, it is common for people to compare their level of spirituality with each other. Some go as far as to boast about their spirituality, like their level of involvement with their church or temple, how much they meditate or pray, or the intensity of their spiritual experiences. More often, however, there is an internal dialogue that occurs among people with the Spirituality addiction where they judge themselves based on their spiritual progress. When they feel they are doing well or are "on track," they feel acceptable, but when they fail to meet their spiritual ideals, they feel guilty and unworthy of love.

The pressure to move forward on a spiritual path comes from our need to prove that we are good enough. It comes from our belief that we are not worthy of love as we are. Although many spiritual organizations claim that climbing to the top of their spiritual ladders will result in ultimate bliss, any condition we place on our self-acceptance results in a never-ending climb to justify our worthiness of love.

An Example of the Spirituality Addiction:

Ursula is an example of a woman who has a Spirituality addiction. She has always considered herself a spiritual person. Through much reading and reflection she has concluded that in order to be more spiritual she needs to be more compassionate to other people. As part of her spiritual routine she meditates and prays daily, while trying to free herself from any negative feelings towards others. Whenever she judges other people, Ursula feels guilty for letting herself down. Here is how Ursula broke down her addiction:

Central → Conditional Love Belief (CCLB):	Conditional → Love Response (CLR):	Conditional → Love Need (CLN):	Conditional Love Action (CLA):
I am not worthy of love and acceptance as I am.	I believe that I am more worthy of love and acceptance when I am spiritual.	I need to be more compassionate towards other people.	I will pray and meditate daily. I will control my negative feelings towards others.

Ursula originally started praying and meditating with the sole intention of being compassionate to others. Despite this intention, somewhere along the way, her level of compassion became a measure of her worth. This is how her addiction began. Now whenever she is not compassionate, she criticizes herself and feels less worthy of acceptance. To avoid these feelings, she tries to stop judging others, even if that means repressing her true feelings. The Spirituality addiction forces Ursula to feel guilty whenever she has emotions that contradict her spiritual ideals. Consequently, she has learned to push aside any emotions that are deemed undesirable. By repressing her feelings, Ursula is not free to be herself, and is not aware of what is really happening within her mind and heart. The deeper connection with herself is severed making it more difficult to access spiritual insights. Do you see the irony of her Spirituality addiction? The very pursuit of her spiritual ideals is preventing her spiritual growth. Her desire to be compassionate has become a source of stress. For this reason, the Spirituality addiction is also one of the most subtle addictions. Most of us are not aware of its presence because we find it difficult to understand how our search for self-fulfillment can be destructive. Yet, unless something is done, the belief that you are not worthy of love as you are will remain the biggest obstacle to your spiritual development.

Questions for Reflection:

1) In your opinion, what makes someone a spiritual person?

2) When you cannot live up to your own ideas of what it is to be a spiritual person, how does this make you feel?

3) Do you feel that you must act a certain way in order to be spiritual? If so, how does this inhibit your personal freedom?

If you can relate to some of the problems that arise in this addiction or find that it limits your freedom in any way, simply check the *My Confirmed Addictions* box for the Spirituality addiction on page 51.

Satyam's Corner
GETTING OUT OF MY OWN WAY

The Spirituality addiction is of particular interest to me because for years it consumed much of my time and energy. I was very young when I first became interested in the spiritual practices of various traditions. Over the years, I cherished the experiences these alternative ways of thinking allowed me to access, and became hooked on them. I began to believe that I needed to have spiritual experiences to feel better about myself. Whenever I did something spiritual, I thought I was acting from my *higher* self and gave myself permission to feel good. And whenever I did something unspiritual, I thought it came from my *lower* self and felt frustrated.

By dividing myself in this fashion, I turned my life into a battlefield. I was convinced that my higher self would eventually win the battle. Later, I realized this could never happen because the moment I started basing my self-acceptance on being spiritual, I was caught in an addiction. The end result was a never-ending need to live up to my spiritual ideals, which prevented me from being in tune with who I was. When I started to break free from the belief that I needed to prove my worth, I was able to enjoy the freedom to discover what spirituality meant to me.

THE GREAT EXPECTATIONS ADDICTION

Do you have expectations of the people close to you? How do you feel when they do not live up to your expectations? Do you feel embarrassed, hurt or upset? Most of us have ideas about how other people should live their lives. Yet, where do these expectations come from, and why does it bother us when people do not live up to them? In many cases, understanding the Great Expectations addiction can provide the answers to these questions.

You have the Great Expectations addiction when you base some of your worthiness of love on whether other people conform to your expectations of them.

The Great Expectations addiction arises from feeling that certain people are extensions of ourselves. In essence, we view them to represent us, and when they let us down our self-worth becomes threatened.

An Example of the Great Expectations Addiction:

John is embarrassed by his wife's behavior in public. He finds her too open about her emotions. This makes him feel uncomfortable because he is concerned about what others might think of her. When he confronts his wife about this, she explains that she is only being herself and expressing her feelings. John keeps demanding that she stop, and his wife resents his need to control her.

Though John genuinely cares about how others perceive his wife, his embarrassment arises from feeling that his wife represents him. When people reject her, he feels that they have rejected him. To protect his reputation, John seeks to control her behavior.

AWARENESS

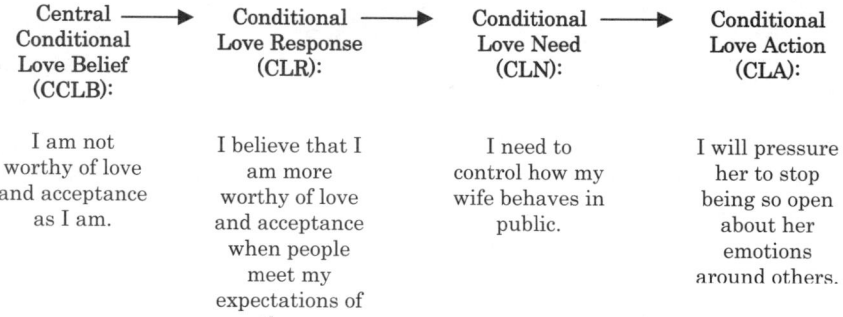

John's Great Expectations addiction is rooted in the belief that he is not worthy of love as he is. In this particular case, John bases his self-acceptance on whether his wife makes a favorable impression on others. When people approve of her, it makes John feel better about himself. She has become an extension of his self-worth. That is why anything she does to jeopardize her image will always be perceived as a threat to John's self-esteem. He is no longer free to accept himself unless she meets his expectations. As a result, John needs to control his wife's behavior to continue feeling acceptable.

Behind the Best of Intentions

Though our expectations can come from the best of intentions, they often reflect our own personal needs and have little to do with the person we expect things from. Another common example of the Great Expectations addiction occurs when parents put pressure on their children to make certain life decisions, such as the career they should pursue or the person they should marry. Parents often feel they are advocating what is in their children's best interest, but many do not take the time to deeply understand the unique needs and desires of their children.

To really understand what is best for another human being is a complicated matter. It takes a great deal of awareness and soul-searching to know what is best for ourselves, let alone to know what is best for someone else. Without taking the time to understand their children, parents can make the mistake of assuming that their children want what they want and start to dangle expectations over their children's heads. Upon further reflection, however, Great Expectations addicts often uncover that their expectations primarily serve to preserve their own reputation and sense of self-acceptance.

Victims of Our Expectations

Ironically, when we have this addiction we may feel victimized by those who do not fulfill our expectations. We may feel that they are deliberately hurting us, but what we tend to ignore is that our expectations can cause just as much pain to them. These expectations can hurt other people by telling them that they will not be accepted unless they fulfill our requirements. The pressure that our expectations impose can also prevent people from sharing their true feelings with us because they fear disappointing us.

Since Great Expectations addicts get upset and frustrated by other people's behavior, they can make the mistake of assuming that changing other people is the solution to their problems. However, most people who disappoint a Great Expectations addict are completely innocent. They have done nothing but express themselves as they saw fit. Great Expectations addicts do not realize that their real problem lies in their belief that they are not worthy of love as they are. Imposing their expectations on others is just another way of trying to fulfill their need to prove their worth.

If people with this addiction put pressure on you to meet their expectations, be careful. You may innocently think that you will eventually meet their needs and make them happy. But, their addiction will never end, and neither will their expectations of you. To break free from this addiction, the most important issue that Great Expectations addicts must address is their inability to accept themselves. When they learn to accept themselves, they will start to understand and support the people they care for, rather than making these people victims of their expectations.

Questions for Reflection:

1) Do you have expectations of other people? If so, who are these people and what are your expectations?

2) What effect do your expectations have on these people?

3) How do you feel when people do not live up to your expectations of them?

4) Is there anything you are doing to make people live up to your expectations?

If you can relate to some of the problems that arise in this addiction or find that it limits your freedom in any way, simply check the *My Confirmed Addictions* box for the Great Expectations addiction on page 51.

THE CONQUEST ADDICTION

There is no subject that arouses as much interest or embarrassment as sex. At one extreme, society exploits and glorifies sex. The media and mainstream culture tend to glamorize sexual conquest. Not surprisingly many of us believe that we need to have sex, and lots of it, in order to live a complete life. Sex, in these cases, has become a means of validating our self-esteem and if we are not having enough of it we can feel there is something seriously missing from our lives.

At another extreme, many religions and cultures are sexually conservative and encourage chastity. They reinforce the message that we should feel guilty or deny our sexual desires. Subject to such contradicting messages, it is no wonder that many of us struggle with conflicting feelings about sex. Although we are not condemning either extreme, it is important to understand how these views are affecting you and to evaluate whether your self-worth depends on living up to either standard.

> **You have the Conquest addiction if you base your worthiness of acceptance on either having many sexual experiences or refraining from sexual experiences.**

Those who have been conditioned to view sex as a means of affirming themselves will seek sexual experiences to prove their worth. Those who have been conditioned to revere abstinence will need to avoid sexual experiences to feel worthy of acceptance.

The Pressure to Perform

If you feel the pressure to have many sexual experiences, you may also experience pressure related to sexual performance. Again, the influence of the media on our attitude towards sex plays a big role in creating this unnecessary stress in our lives. The next time you are in the check-out line of a supermarket, take a moment to peruse the magazine rack and notice how often sex is mentioned. One of the hottest topics discussed in these magazines is how to sexually satisfy your partner. There is no doubt that sex sells, but how is this emphasis on sexual performance affecting our attitude toward sex? For people with the Conquest addiction, the pressure to perform often surfaces. This pressure can come from trying to meet their own ideas of what it is to be sexually competent, or it may come from the sexual expectations their partners may have of them. Not only does the addiction limit our freedom to enjoy sexual experiences, but the performance anxiety can even result in sexual dysfunction.

An Example of the Conquest Addiction:

Oscar seeks sexual experiences with women he finds attractive, and whenever he succeeds, he experiences a sense of triumph that comes from validating his worth. It is not long, however, before he wants to sleep with another woman to fulfill his need to feel sexually competent.

Central Conditional Love Belief (CCLB):	Conditional Love Response (CLR):	Conditional Love Need (CLN):	Conditional Love Action (CLA):
I am not worthy of love and acceptance as I am.	I believe that I am more worthy of love and acceptance when I have sexual experiences with women.	I need to sleep with many women.	I will try to seduce many women.
		I need to perform well in bed.	I will try to perform well in bed.

As long as Oscar can live up to the demands of his addiction, he can continue to feel good about himself. But, what happens to Oscar when he is unable to seduce women into sleeping with him? How will he feel if a woman does not approve of his sexual performance? He will begin to question his worthiness of love, and this will lead to stress or anxiety in his life. To avoid the withdrawal symptoms of his addiction, he will feel a need to re-establish his sense of worth. Oscar's addiction has made him attach the one thing he wants more than anything, love and acceptance, to his sex life. Consequently, to feel worthy of acceptance again, he needs to prove his sexual competence through having more conquests. Like all CLS Addictions, the emotional high he gets from satisfying his addiction has a strong influence in making him want more. When you combine this with the actual physical pleasure that he experiences during sex, the Conquest addiction has an even greater power over his life.

Questions for Reflection:

If you can relate to the need to have many sexual experiences answer the following questions:

1. Do you feel it is important to have many sexual experiences? If so, why?

2. Do you feel any pressure to perform well in bed?

3. Are you doing anything to get people to sleep with you?

If you can relate to the need to refrain from sexual experiences answer the following questions:

1. Do you feel it is important to abstain from sexual experiences? If so, why?

2. Does your opinion of yourself change when you have a sexual experience? If so, how?

3. Are you doing anything to avoid having sexual experiences?

If you can relate to some of the problems that arise in this addiction or find that it limits your freedom in any way, simply check the *My Confirmed Addictions* box for the Conquest addiction on page 51.

The Productivity Addiction

Do you feel frustrated with yourself when you cannot get enough done in a day? Do you like to make *to-do* lists and get a thrill out of checking things off? If so, pay special attention to this addiction. It can be a major source of stress in your life.

> **You have the Productivity addiction when you believe that you must be productive before you can feel completely acceptable.**

In our fast-paced world, people are busier than ever before. There is definitely nothing wrong with trying to accomplish many things. However, when you develop the Productivity addiction, the way you feel about yourself depends on whether you have been successful in meeting the demands of your life.

A Race Against the Clock

George is an example of a very active man who prides himself on being productive. He pushes himself to accomplish many things each day, even on holidays. He cannot understand why people waste their time and feels uncomfortable whenever he is forced to do trivial things like standing in line or waiting for friends. Throughout the day he gets satisfaction from crossing items off his to-do list. At the same time, if he does not achieve enough each day, George cannot help but feel frustrated with himself.

Central Conditional Love Belief (CCLB):	⟶	Conditional Love Response (CLR):	⟶	Conditional Love Need (CLN):	⟶	Conditional Love Action (CLA):
I am not worthy of love and acceptance as I am.		I believe that I am more worthy of love and acceptance when I am productive.		I need to make every day productive.		I will work hard to do everything on my to-do list. I will not relax until my tasks are completed.

As with all addictions, George's self-esteem is connected to fulfilling a condition. In his case, that condition is being productive. With his CLR, he does not just want to be productive, he needs to be productive. Whenever he is not as productive as he intends to be, he cannot accept himself. The only time George can allow himself to feel relaxed is when he is assured of accomplishing everything he planned. Consequently, he often feels like he is racing against the clock. But his race has no finish line. As long as George has this addiction, no matter how much he does today, he will need to be just as productive tomorrow. Often, George can become so consumed in trying to get things done that he is unable to enjoy the process. Though he recognizes this problem, he cannot help himself. Since George feels unworthy of love as he is, he will be compelled to remain focused on achieving as much as he can.

The need for productivity can affect us even when we have scheduled the time to relax with family and friends. Unable to turn off our productivity mode, we often find ourselves stressing over the things we have to do later, at the expense of enjoying ourselves right now. Defining ourselves by what we do keeps us running on fifth gear most of the time. Pushing ourselves to prove our worth in this manner can force us to sacrifice the moments we would rather be cherishing.

Considering how much society values productivity, it is not surprising to see how prevalent this addiction is. To appreciate the importance we place on productivity, just reflect on your typical conversations with people. Some of the first questions we ask each other are: "What are you doing tonight?" "What did you do over the weekend?" Or a personal favorite: "What countries did you do during your travels?" Usually these are harmless conversation starters, but who can argue against the fact that we are often judged by our responses to these questions. When we believe that we are not worthy of love as we are, we internalize these judgments and base our self-acceptance on doing as much as we can. The result is that we must cope with the frequent bouts of stress that arise from the Productivity addiction.

LIVING FOR ANOTHER DAY

Amidst the pressure to be productive, the quality of our life experiences is often sacrificed for a greater quantity of experiences. It is as if we are trying to total up what we have done at the end of each day and cash that in for a greater sense of self-worth. People apply this mentality to their entire lives as well; they strive to do as much as they can, hoping that it will all be worth it in the end. They imagine that on their deathbed they will be able to look back on all their achievements with pride. However, this perspective can make us sacrifice the journey for the destination. By living for the future, we can lose today and the moments that make up our lives.

Questions for Reflection:

1) What do you consider to be a productive use of your time?

2) How do you feel when you are not productive?

3) How is the pressure to be productive affecting your daily activities?

If you can relate to some of the problems that arise in this addiction or find that it limits your freedom in any way, simply check the *My Confirmed Addictions* box for the Productivity addiction on page 51.

Freedom's Corner
LETTING GO OF THE NEED TO BE PRODUCTIVE

At work, the pressure to be productive is very real. People risk losing their jobs if they do not meet deadlines or reach goals. As a result, most employees are motivated to work very hard because they fear what might happen to them if they are not productive enough.

I know a recently retired senior executive of a major multinational corporation who serendipitously came upon an intriguing discovery. In his last year of working for the company, his seniority assured him absolute job security. Consequently, for the first time, he decided not to concern himself with being too productive that year.

To his surprise, he achieved more in that final year of work than he did in any year of his entire career. The special circumstances surrounding his final year before retirement allowed this executive to let go of his Productivity addiction, and thereby stumble upon a deep truth:

Freedom from the need to be productive empowers you with the clarity and energy that is otherwise lost in the fear of being unproductive.

By letting go of his need to be productive, the executive armed himself with a greater presence of mind. This gave him the freedom to focus on whatever task was in front of him, rather than wasting his time and energy worrying about whether he would complete the task or not. In turn, the quality and efficiency of his work improved significantly.

The Criticism Addiction

Can you think of someone who is very critical of others? How does this person make you feel when you are in his or her presence? Most of us feel uneasy around those who constantly point out our flaws. Nonetheless, we all engage in criticizing people from time to time. Have you ever considered where this need to criticize others comes from? Often we criticize others out of a need to protect ourselves from feelings of insecurity. It is a defense mechanism against anything that threatens our acceptability. We point out the shortcomings of others as a means of coping with our own sense of inadequacy. It is as if we find comfort and consolation in convincing ourselves that there are at least other people who are less acceptable than we are. The Criticism addiction helps explain why we feel the need to do this.

If you need to put other people down in order to feel better about yourself, you have the Criticism addiction.

Criticism can be constructive when the intent is to offer suggestions for improvement. However, most criticism is destructive. It is conveyed with either the conscious or subconscious intent of belittling another to bolster one's own ego. This is because finding flaws is one of the ways we have learned to feel superior to those we find threatening. Yet, when we take a good look at what we are doing, we will realize that this act of criticism is not healthy. Though it may offer temporary comfort, it is also a draining process because it does not address the root cause of why we feel insecure in the first place. The temporary satisfaction we get from putting others down is often accompanied with frustration because something else is bothering us deep down. For this reason, the energy we waste in criticizing others could be put to much better use by trying to figure out what is making us feel less acceptable in the first place.

The Criticism Addiction Distracts You from the Deeper Problem

Ray is an example of someone who has the Criticism addiction. For the longest time he has dreamt of becoming a screenwriter. Though he has a full-time job, he dedicates his free time to writing in the hope of eventually turning one of his stories into a feature film. Unfortunately, after three years of writing, he has been unsuccessful in attracting the attention of any production studio. Ray never thought it would take so long to sell his work. In the past, Ray loved to watch movies, but now he is quick to find flaws in every storyline.

Central Conditional Love Belief (CCLB):	→	Conditional Love Response (CLR):	→	Conditional Love Need (CLN):	→	Conditional Love Action (CLA):
I am not worthy of love and acceptance as I am.		I believe that I am more worthy of acceptance when I can prove others are less worthy of acceptance.		I need to criticize the works of other successful screenwriters to help me avoid feeling like a failure.		I will go out of my way to find flaws in the movies I watch.

Criticism addictions are invariably coupled with another addiction. Behind Ray's Criticism addiction is a Success Addiction. Ray feels that he is more worthy of love when he is a successful screenwriter. Since he has not been able to succeed as a screenwriter, Ray criticizes to avoid feeling like a failure and, therefore, less worthy of love. Though finding flaws in others may make him feel a little better about himself, deep down he will continue to feel inadequate until he becomes successful. However, even if Ray achieves this goal, his dissatisfaction will return. Ray's Success addiction will demand that he keep proving himself through one achievement after another.

The key thing for Ray to understand is that criticizing others is futile. The addiction only takes his energy away from addressing his deeper frustration of being unsuccessful. Once he understands this, trying to satisfy his Success addiction will also be futile. Satisfying these addictions only distracts him from the deepest problem. Ray believes that he is unworthy of love as he is. Until he takes the time to look inside of himself and break free from this belief, no amount of success or criticism will give him the freedom to accept himself.

Questions for Reflection:

1) Do you tend to criticize other people? If so, what is it that you are critical about?

2) Does criticizing other people make you feel better about yourself?

3) Is your need to criticize compensating for a feeling of inadequacy in your life?

If you can relate to some of the problems that arise in this addiction or find that it limits your freedom in any way, simply check the *My Confirmed Addictions* box for the Criticism addiction on page 51.

Understanding Your CLS Addictions

So far you have been introduced to the CLS and confirmed which of the twelve major CLS Addictions you have. The work you have done to this point has built an important foundation of knowledge. However, this is just the beginning. In the next three exercises, you will investigate in more detail how these addictions are specifically influencing your life. This in-depth exploration will allow you to appreciate how real these addictions are, their impact on your emotional state, and their influence on your behavior. Only by taking the time to evaluate your addictions through the following exercises can you understand the true significance of the belief that you are not worthy of love as you are and its potential to dominate your life.

Three At A Time:

At this stage, you are not advised to analyze all your addictions at once because that can be both overwhelming and cumbersome. To start off, try all the exercises in this book on three of your addictions. Choose the three addictions that you feel have the greatest influence on your life. Having selected your three addictions, you are now ready to begin the process of exploring each of them in depth.

Recalling Addictive Behaviors

The purpose of this exercise is to recognize when your addictions affect you. To do this, you are going to recall incidents where each addiction came up in your life. For example, if you have an Appearance addiction, you might remember a time when you were self-conscious about your body. If you have the Acceptance of Others addiction, you may recall when your need for the acceptance of someone prevented you from expressing yourself. If you have the Comparison addiction, you may recollect a time you felt insecure around someone with whom you compared yourself.

Try to recall at least two or three experiences for each addiction. The more you remember, the more thorough your investigation will be. Complete the following steps for each of the incidents you have selected:

1) Close your eyes and imagine yourself reliving the experience. Try to visualize every detail as if it were happening again right before your own eyes.

2) To prompt your recollection of each experience, ask yourself the following questions: "What was I doing? What was I thinking? What was I feeling?"

3) Record the details on a piece of paper.

While doing this exercise, it is important that you imagine yourself going through the actual experience. The more vividly you recall each incident, the more accurate your assessment will be. Think of each incident as a scene from the movie of your life. Replay the incident in your mind while reflecting on the actual thoughts, feelings, and actions that took place.

While recollecting each incident, try not to censor any of the information or condemn any of your thoughts or feelings. Again, the purpose of this exercise is to become more aware of how your addictions are influencing you. Since you have only been asked to observe what happened, judging yourself has no place in this process.

For examples of this exercise, please refer to the next page.

Please note that if some of the events in your past are too painful to recall or if this exercise becomes too intense, we recommend that you do not vividly recall those events at this time. The purpose of this exercise is to become aware of what you were experiencing during these incidents, *not* to cause further emotional trauma.

A Helpful Tip

Since you will be extensively examining each incident in the exercises to follow, it is highly recommended that you explore each incident on a separate sheet of paper. This tip will save you from having to rewrite your thoughts.

RECALLING ADDICTIVE BEHAVIORS – EXAMPLE 1

<u>Addiction:</u> **Acceptance of Others**

> <u>Incident:</u> Last week I was out with a couple of close friends playing golf. Although I was upset over certain home and work-related matters, I pretended like everything was alright. My friends have always admired me for my achievements. I have managed to uphold this image of having the perfect life with a great job and family. And though my life is far from perfect, I found myself trying to keep that image alive at the golf course. At times it felt like I was looking at myself through their eyes, and I wanted them to keep admiring me. Their admiration made me feel a little better about myself, but it also made it hard for me to reveal my true thoughts and feelings around them. I was afraid they would see me as a failure if I shared my vulnerabilities with them.

RECALLING ADDICTIVE BEHAVIORS – EXAMPLE 2

<u>Addiction:</u> **Comparison**

> <u>Incident:</u> A while ago, I was at a party and met someone who began telling me about his successful career. He told me about how he owned several apartment buildings and managed numerous businesses. While he was talking I found myself comparing my own achievements and wealth with his. Though I have always been fairly content with my job, I started to feel insecure around him. As the conversation went on, I felt less and less good about myself. I have to admit I felt slightly jealous around him as well. Since this party, I have been trying to think of ways that I could make more money, or become more successful at work. To avoid feeling more insecure about myself, I try to avoid bumping into him at other gatherings.

BREAKING DOWN YOUR ADDICTIONS

In this next exercise, you will be breaking down each incident you recalled into the four components of an addiction. The purpose of this exercise is to understand the thought process that is behind your addictions. By determining the beliefs, needs, and actions that make up your addictions, you will understand exactly how your addictions stem from one central belief.

We have thousands of thoughts every day. From this, it is reasonable to assume that you had dozens, perhaps even hundreds of thoughts during each incident you recalled in the previous exercise. It is important to realize that not all thoughts are equal. Some of your thoughts are almost insignificant, while others determine your experience of life. Breaking down your addictions into their respective components helps you determine your most influential thoughts and the role they play in your life. This process will help you gain remarkable insight into the connections between your thoughts, feelings, and actions. You will also learn to appreciate how much of your life is being influenced by the belief that you are not worthy of love as you are.

When breaking down your addictions, it often helps to work backwards starting from the Conditional Love Action (CLA). However, it all comes down to preference. You can also experiment with working forwards from the Central Conditional Love Belief (CCLB).

The following steps illustrate how to work backwards. Complete the steps for each of the incidents you identified in the previous exercise.

1) Start by describing your Conditional Love Action (CLA). To do this, determine what you did to prove your worth. To help express this in words begin with the phrase "I will." In an earlier example with Rachel's Success addiction (page 55), we identified her CLAs to be "I will work harder," "I will work longer hours," and "I will sacrifice time with my family to get this promotion."

2) Now work backwards to describe the Conditional Love Need (CLN). To do this, determine what need your action attempted to

satisfy. To help express this in words begin with the phrase "I need." With Rachel's Success addiction, her CLN was "I need to get the job promotion."

3) Now work backwards to describe the Conditional Love Response (CLR). To do this, determine what belief creates the Conditional Love Need. To help express this in words begin with the phrase "I believe I am more worthy of love and acceptance when." If you recall, with Rachel's Success addiction her CLR was: "I believe that I am more worthy of love and acceptance when I am successful."

4) Complete the process by writing down the Central Conditional Love Belief (CCLB) of "I am not worthy of love and acceptance as I am." Observe how all addictions arise from this central belief.

Keep in mind that this is not meant to be an entirely cerebral process. Try to access your emotions as they often hold the key to valuable insights. Also, note that it is possible for you to have more than one need (CLN) or action (CLA) for each incident.

"Know Thyself"

Breaking Down Your Addictions takes time and concerted effort. Yet, it is one of the most rewarding exercises. This is an opportunity to reflect upon your past and understand yourself from an entirely different perspective. There's no need to rush the process. Consider this time to be an investment into understanding yourself.

For examples of this exercise, please refer to the next page. The examples provided are based on the incidents described earlier in the Recalling Addictive Behaviors exercise.

BREAKING DOWN YOUR ADDICTIONS – EXAMPLE 1

Addiction: Acceptance of Others

Central⟶ Conditional Love Belief (CCLB):	Conditional⟶ Love Response (CLR):	Conditional⟶ Love Need (CLN):	Conditional Love Action (CLA):
I am not worthy of love and acceptance as I am.	I believe that I am more worthy of love and acceptance when I gain the approval of others.	I need my friends to accept and approve of me.	I will try to maintain an image of being successful at work and home so my friends will continue to admire me.

BREAKING DOWN YOUR ADDICTIONS – EXAMPLE 2

Addiction: Comparison

Central⟶ Conditional Love Belief (CCLB):	Conditional⟶ Love Response (CLR):	Conditional⟶ Love Need (CLN):	Conditional Love Action (CLA):
I am not worthy of love and acceptance as I am.	I believe that I am more worthy of love and acceptance when I am better than others.	I need to be more wealthy and successful than the person I met at the party.	I will strive to achieve more. I will try to steer clear of this person so that I can avoid the feelings of insecurity that he evokes in me.

Experiencing Withdrawal

In the context of a substance addiction, *withdrawal* is the physical and psychological reaction that occurs when you stop satisfying an addiction. For example, heroin users can feel restless, anxious and irritable when the drug is withheld from them. Similarly, you will experience your own set of withdrawal symptoms every time you are unable to satisfy any of your CLS Addictions.

In this exercise, you will simulate the experience of withdrawal for each of the addictions you are examining. By doing this exercise, you will appreciate how powerful your need to fulfill addictions is and how much of a grip the CCLB has on your life. This is important to experience so that you fully grasp the nature of the CLS and why these behaviors have been appropriately described as addictions.

For this exercise to be effective, it is important that you do your best to imagine how you would feel if you could no longer fulfill the needs (CLNs) that each addiction requires of you. For instance, if your Success addiction creates a need for a successful career, you would imagine how it would feel if you could not fulfill this need and were a complete failure. Similarly, if your Acceptance of Others addiction creates a need for the approval of your father, you will imagine how you would feel if you lost his acceptance. If you have the Appearance addiction, imagine how it would feel if you are no longer attractive. Imagining some of these things will not be easy, but it will be worth the effort. Remember, it is not enough to philosophize over how you might feel. You need to really go there in your mind and heart. Try to fully visualize yourself in the situation and let yourself experience the emotions it evokes.

Complete these steps for each addiction that you broke down in the previous exercise:

1) Imagine that you cannot satisfy the Conditional Love Needs (CLNs) that relate to your addiction.

2) Write down the thoughts and feelings that run through your mind as you experience this situation.

Experiencing Withdrawal – Example

Here are the notes of someone who completed this exercise. She imagined herself failing at something very important to her.

> When I imagine myself failing, I feel my breathing becoming shallow and body slouching over. I begin to feel awful. I try to come up with ways of resolving the situation. When that does not work I struggle to accept my failure. I feel myself resisting this process because it is very difficult for me to accept that I have failed. It feels like a big blow to my confidence. I try to come up with excuses for why the defeat was not my fault. I start to consider what other people might think and how they would probably look down on me for failing. I want to explain to each one of them what happened and how it is not my fault. I start to console myself by remembering all the things I achieved in the past. I try to restore my hopes by thinking about all the things I will still be able to achieve in the future. This helps calm me down a little bit.

As long as we have addictions, we will continue to reach for our *fix* in any way we can to avoid the discomfort of withdrawal symptoms. In the above example, notice how she tries at first to rectify the situation, then to make an excuse for the failure, and then finally she manages to comfort herself by resolving to succeed in the future. Each of her reactions illustrates how the intense need to fulfill our addictions can dictate our behavior.

In the next section, you will further explore the enslaving consequences of staying addicted.

The Web Of Slavery

The more you study the role addictions play in your life, the more you will appreciate how much of an impact the CCLB can have on your freedom. Addictions become even more fascinating when you examine how they work together. To help illustrate this, let's take the example of Carlos and his four dominant addictions as depicted by the diagram on the following page. The diagram shows how these addictions play out in Carlos' life. The CCLB of "I am not worthy of love and acceptance as I am" is at the center. This is the starting point of all addictions. In Carlos' case, the following four addictions arise from the CCLB: Acceptance of Others, Comparison, Great Expectations, and Success. These are depicted in the first circle around the CCLB. Within each addiction, Carlos has many needs to satisfy. The diagram illustrates the needs that are related to each addiction and are found in the second circle around the CCLB. Examining addictions together in this fashion will help take your awareness of the CLS to another level. When you are done reading about Carlos we highly recommend examining your own addictions in this way as well.

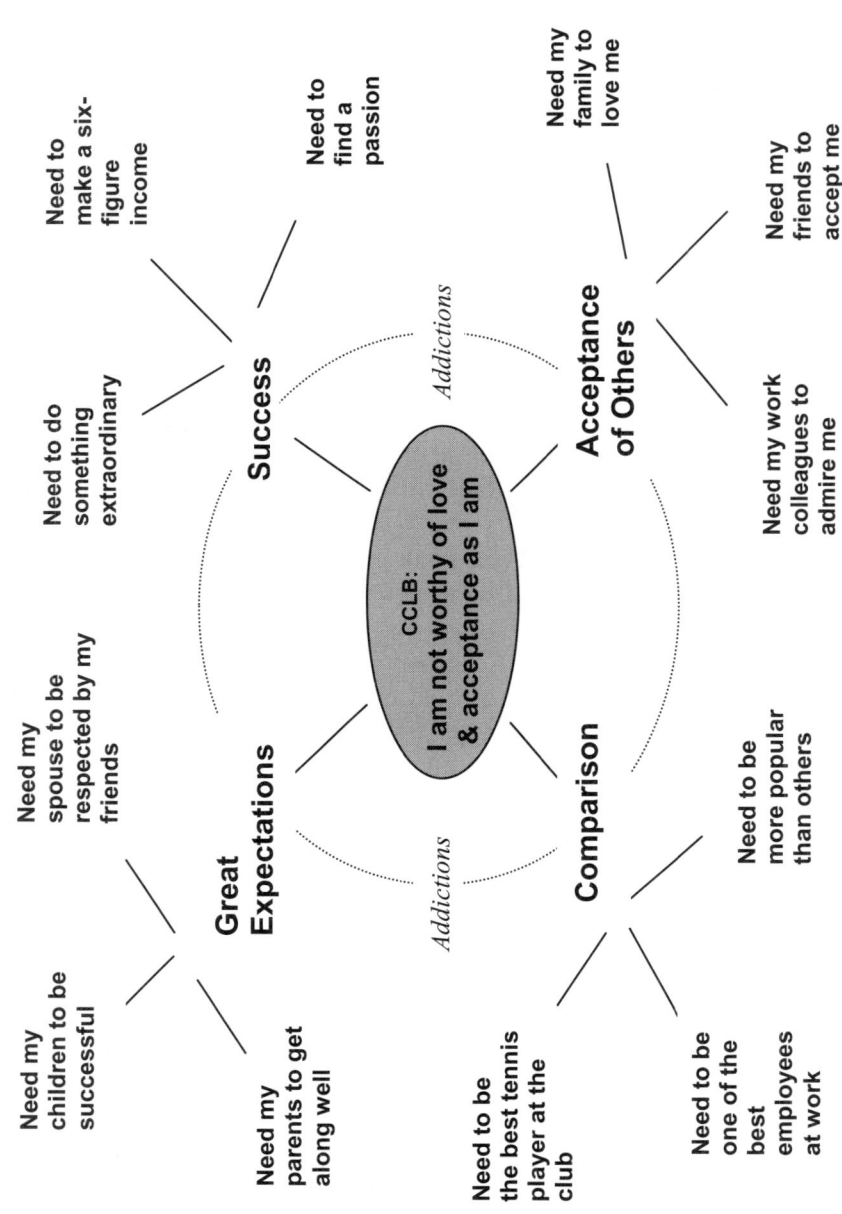

Here are some of the insights revealed through Carlos' CLS:

In the CLS, feeling completely worthy of love and acceptance becomes an almost impossible task.

When you examine Carlos' CLS, it is amazing to observe how many needs are created from one central belief (the CCLB). Each of these needs has a power over Carlos because his self-worth is dependent on fulfilling them. Whenever these needs are not met, Carlos cannot feel good about himself. For example, if he loses the acceptance of his friends, or his children are not successful, his justification for feeling worthy of acceptance will be compromised. With so many needs arising from the CCLB, it is very difficult for Carlos to accept himself. Our lives are no different. Just think about your own experiences. How often do you feel totally acceptable? How often do you give yourself permission to feel completely good about who you are? When you examine the many needs of your own CLS, it will become clear why it can be so difficult to be content. The addictions create so many needs for us to satisfy that we usually feel that something is missing from our lives.

Your CLS Addictions create a web that eliminates the possibility of freedom.

Being in the CLS is not always a dreary experience for Carlos. There are times when he feels completely acceptable. In fact, when he manages to fulfill most of his CLNs, Carlos can even feel on top of the world. Unfortunately, these experiences are short-lived because it will not be long before one of his addictions is challenged. For example, if Carlos notices that a colleague is doing better than he is at work, he will feel threatened because of his Comparison addiction. No matter how good he is feeling, this single challenge is usually enough to put his self-worth in jeopardy. To avoid feeling unacceptable, Carlos will then feel compelled to push himself harder at work.

When you look closely at the diagram, you will notice that it looks similar to a spider web. Being in the CLS feels like living in a web, a fragile web that must be maintained throughout our lives. Any time one of our addictions is challenged, part of this web breaks. Just as a spider must repair its web when it is broken, we must scramble to fix the CLS web by addressing whichever addiction needs to be satisfied.

Since the web is fragile so, too, is our peace of mind. For example, when Carlos loses the acceptance of a few colleagues, he will feel a mounting tension in his life until he can regain his popularity. When his spouse is not respected by a circle of friends, he will again feel some anxiety until he can find a way to resolve the situation. Each of us has our own unique web made from the many beliefs, needs, and actions of our addictions. We may not always be conscious of it, but our ability to satisfy the needs of the web heavily influences how we feel at any given moment. The result is that, whether our addictions are fulfilled or not, most of our time and energy is still spent ensuring that the web stays intact.

To make matters worse, the so-called needs of the CLS are not real needs. They only exist because we have been led to believe they are necessary to feel worthy of love. Nevertheless, we may become so preoccupied with fulfilling all these needs that we do not have a chance to look within to uncover what we really want.

The motivation in the CLS is based on fear.

The experience of feeling unworthy of love can be so painful that it creates fear in our lives. The fear of not being able to prove our worth is what motivates each of us to fulfill our CLS Addictions. No doubt, fear has its benefits. If we are in physical danger, it has an important role in eliciting our fight or flight mechanism. Physiologically we become prepared to do what is necessary in an emergency. Fortunately, we are rarely under the threat of physical danger. Yet, being unable to fulfill an addiction in the CLS can have the same effect on us because it is a threat to our self-worth. For some of us, the fear can be very intense, while for others, it can play a more subtle role in the backgrounds of our lives. In either case, our fear is not pleasant, and, in the long run, the stress our minds and bodies endure from the CLS can be a major contributing factor to health problems.

At the same time, fear clouds the mind and drastically reduces our effectiveness in completing any task. Most people who have achieved anything will agree that when they are calm their performance is enhanced. If you have ever played sports competitively, you know that your body tightens up whenever you are afraid, and this takes away from your performance. Whereas, when you are relaxed, you are free to flow and play far more effectively. Though fear can certainly motivate us to fulfill our addictions, it is unnecessary, and its negative effect on our physical health and performance can prevent us from doing the things we want.

It is important to stress that all of the fear we experience through our addictions arises because of the CCLB. Our fear of not being worthy of acceptance only comes from the belief that we must prove our worth. For this reason, addictions and their power over our lives depend entirely on the presence of the CCLB. That is why our search for self-acceptance and the fear we experience through our addictions cannot end until we challenge this central belief.

Any Condition Will Enslave You

As we conclude The Web of Slavery, one observation must be emphasized:

Any idea of what you need to become to feel more worthy of love will become an addiction that enslaves you.

Even if you place only one condition on your acceptability it will lead to the slavery of an addiction and limit your freedom. Study this point and it will save you from spending years chasing after fulfillment where it cannot be found.

Now that you have an appreciation for the Web of Slavery, you may wonder if there is a way to live free from the CLS and the limitations imposed by addictions. Is there a way to feel good about ourselves without having to prove our worth? Are there other motivations that can push us towards our goals besides fear? How can we free our time and energy to uncover what we really want? We will explore the answers to these questions and many others in the remaining pages of the Awareness section. But, first you must learn about *The Personal Freedom Rule*. This rule will empower you with a greater understanding of central beliefs and set the stage for the exercises to come.

Beliefs Are Powerful And Can Be Changed

Central beliefs have a tremendous influence on how our lives unfold.

> ### The Personal Freedom Rule
>
> **Changing a central belief will result in change across many aspects of your life.**

When it comes to reclaiming your freedom, the implications of the above statement are essential to understand. That is why it is called The Personal Freedom Rule. This rule not only applies to individuals, but also to societies. A change in the central beliefs of a society will result in a transformation in the way that society functions. There are countless instances of such transformations in history. For example, not so long ago the belief that males were superior to females was widely accepted in North America. The belief in gender equality, however, has challenged and continues to challenge this sexist belief. Wherever the belief that women are inferior has been replaced with a belief in equality, there has been a dramatic change in the way women are perceived and treated. This has led to the development of new opportunities and lifestyles for women. Such changes shall continue as society deepens its appreciation for gender equality.

In this example it is important to highlight that before society could change, there first had to be a change in the way women perceived themselves. Individually, women revised their own sense of identity and their vision of what they were capable of. This was very challenging considering that practically every message women received reinforced the idea that men were superior. Their parents, their schooling, the media, and everyone they met all reinforced this belief. Despite this conditioning, some women found the courage to break free from this belief by choosing a new identity for themselves. Their struggles eventually led to the Women's Liberation movement and the freedoms many women enjoy today.

In our lives there is another deep-rooted belief that also poses a tremendous limitation on our freedom. It is the belief that we are not worthy of love and acceptance as we are. Just as the belief in gender inequality was a major part of a woman's social conditioning, this belief has been conditioned and reinforced into our minds all our lives. Through your own exploration, you have begun to understand the effects of this belief, and how it is at the root of the fears and insecurities that hold you back in life. You have also begun to see how this belief creates a web of never-ending addictions that pressure you to prove your worthiness of love. As long as women believed they were inferior to men they could never experience the freedom of equality. Similarly, as long as you believe that you are not worthy of love as you are, you cannot begin to realize the freedom that is rightfully yours.

If you wanted to break free from the CLS, where would you begin? During the Women's Liberation movement, the alternative belief was clear. Only gender equality could grant women freedom from the oppressive central belief of their time. But, what is the alternative to the CLS? What is the new central belief that would allow you to break free from the oppression of your addictions? Now that you have thoroughly understood how your freedom has been limited by the CLS, you are in a position to explore what this freedom means to you. It is time to envision new possibilities for your life from a center of complete freedom. At this stage, it is not important to understand how you can make this transformation possible. Just as those who participated in the Women's Liberation movement challenged the central belief of gender inequality, you, too, can choose to challenge the central belief of the CLS. But, first you must dream. First, you must explore the alternative to the CLS and what it means in your life. Then if you want, you can begin to revolutionize your experience of life. So get ready! You are about to discover a state of being that few people know exists and even fewer dare to explore.

Before turning to the next page, take a few moments to close your eyes and consider how your life would change if you believed that:

YOU ARE WORTHY OF LOVE AND ACCEPTANCE AS YOU ARE.

The Unconditional Love State (ULS)

The world we have created is a product of our thinking.
It cannot be changed without changing our thinking.

ALBERT EINSTEIN

When you challenge a central belief, you open the door to new possibilities. You will now consider the benefits of challenging the central belief of the CLS. What will your perspective be if you believe that you are worthy of love as you are? Would you still be seeking the same things from life? How would your day-to-day experiences change? These are just some of the many questions we will explore during your investigation of a totally unique way of living – the Unconditional Love State (ULS). To begin, here is an introduction to some of its primary features.

The ULS is based on the central belief of "I am worthy of love and acceptance as I am."

This central belief can also be expressed as:

"I do not have to prove my worthiness of love and acceptance."
"I do not need a reason to feel good about myself."
"I do not have to validate my self-worth."

Whichever way you choose to describe it, this central belief affirms that you no longer need to do anything to experience the love and acceptance you long for. In other words, you give yourself absolute permission to feel good about yourself regardless of what you do. Remember, in the CLS, you must justify your right to feel good about yourself through fulfilling the conditions of your addictions. This is how we have been taught to experience love, and most of us have accepted this as the only reality. However, it is a reality based entirely on a belief, and it is only real if we choose to believe in it. The ULS reveals a totally different way of experiencing love and acceptance that is accessible to you right now. It empowers you with a way of satisfying your deepest need for love and acceptance that is far more practical and effective than the CLS.

In the ULS there are no more conditions placed on your self-worth. There is no justification required because the central belief declares that you are worthy of love and acceptance as you are. You are free to feel good for no reason whatsoever. Make no mistake about it. The ULS does not say that you should find something admirable about yourself and love yourself because of it. Nor does it say to search for the unique qualities that make you a special person and worthy of love. It is the complete realization that you do not need a single reason to feel good about yourself and that you, with all your so-called flaws, are completely worthy of love.

The ULS gives you the courage to live your life the way you want.

Unfortunately, most people are not aware of the CLS, let alone aware that an alternative as empowering as the ULS exists. As a result, they are forced to spend so much of their time and energy trying to fulfill the needs created by their addictions. When you reclaim the freedom to accept yourself as you are, these needs no longer exist. Yet, this does not mean that you stop doing things. On the contrary, you will uncover the clarity to identify what you really want and the strength to go after it with all your heart.

By going through the process of understanding your CLS Addictions, you can now recognize the chains imposed on your mind and heart. You are now aware that many of your needs arise from a belief that you must prove your worth. With this new awareness you can appreciate just how much liberty the belief that you are worthy of love grants. The central belief of the ULS gives you the freedom to be yourself because it releases you from the need to become or achieve anything. After all, you were not made to be anyone other than yourself. The deepest layers of your being live to nurture the full expression of your authentic self. In the ULS, the decision of how you want to live your life is finally back where it belongs – in your hands.

The ULS helps you break free from your fear and your addictions.

When caught in the web of the CLS, the pressure to satisfy your addictions is endless. As long as you base your self-acceptance on conditions, you will remain addicted. Also, while you struggle to maintain the conditions that keep your CLS web intact, you will continue to fear the circumstances that can threaten your self-worth.

The ULS introduces a completely different approach to life by uprooting the central belief behind your addictions. It gives you the opportunity to establish a new foundation for your life free from the emotional dependence and fear created by the CLS.

Once you decide that you are worthy of love as you are, no circumstance can threaten your self-worth. You are capable of accepting all situations because nothing can take away your self-respect. What people think of you or how they might react is no longer relevant to your self-esteem. The ULS allows you to access a deeper source of confidence that comes from within. This source of confidence is self-sustaining because it is based on a love with no strings attached, a love without any conditions.

In the ULS, you no longer fear being unable to satisfy your addictions because there is nothing left to prove. For example, how can Success addicts continue to fear failure if they know they are worthy of love regardless of whether they succeed? How can Appearance addicts remain self-conscious about their looks when they understand that they are acceptable as they are? What would Criticism addicts have to gain from finding faults in others if they already felt good about themselves? Each addiction falls apart with this new central belief because you have eliminated the need to prove yourself worthy of the love and acceptance you long for.

The ULS opens the door to a new world of possibilities.

Learning how the ULS can affect you is an exciting process because only you can uncover what you will find. The ULS is a new territory for most people, and its exploration is a completely individual experience. In fact, everyone has a different idea of what freedom means to them when they consider the possibility of living without their addictions. By exploring the ULS, you are tapping into a part of yourself that is not afraid and holds the key to a world of new possibilities. That is why we encourage you to take your time while exploring this sacred place within yourself.

After being introduced to the ULS, you may wonder if such a state of being is possible. This is a natural question. For now, don't worry about whether it is possible or not. At this point, simply explore the ULS through the exercises to come. Have fun with them. Let yourself venture into a new frontier and a realm of new possibilities. After this exploration, if you decide to switch from the CLS to the ULS, rest assured that this book will provide you with the tools needed to make it happen.

UNDERSTANDING THE ULS

Before you explore how the ULS can affect your life, it is important to understand how the behaviors in the ULS are broken down into the four following components:

1) **CULB – Central Unconditional Love Belief**

    "I am worthy of love and acceptance as I am" is the central belief of all the behaviors in the ULS.

2) **ULR – Unconditional Love Response**

    These responses express our freedom from the conditions we once placed on loving and accepting ourselves.

3) **ULC – Unconditional Love Choice**

    These choices arise from our Unconditional Love Responses (ULRs). When we free ourselves from the conditions placed on our self-love, we become free to choose how we want to live.

4) **ULA – Unconditional Love Action**

    These actions are intended to fulfill the Unconditional Love Choices we have made.

<u>The Four Components of Behaviors in the ULS</u>

Central Unconditional Love Belief (CULB) → Unconditional Love Response (ULR) → Unconditional Love Choice (ULC) → Unconditional Love Action (ULA)

We will now use a few examples to help illustrate how to apply these concepts. The examples will show how the ULS can be explored by simply replacing the Central Conditional Love Belief

(CCLB) with the Central Unconditional Love Belief (CULB). If you recall from the description of the Acceptance of Others addiction, Curtis believed that he was more worthy of love when his parents approved of his decisions. This led him to give up his passion for music to pursue a career in law (Figure 1A). Here is how Curtis' perspective changed when he explored the possibility of replacing his CCLB with the CULB (Figure 1B).

Figure 1A: Curtis' Conditional Love State Addiction

Central Conditional Love Belief (CCLB):	→	Conditional Love Response (CLR):	→	Conditional Love Need (CLN):	→	Conditional Love Action (CLA):
I am not worthy of love and acceptance as I am.		I believe that I am more worthy of love and acceptance when I am accepted by others.		I need my parents to accept my career decision.		I will become a lawyer to gain my parent's approval.

Figure 1B: Curtis' Behavior in the ULS

Central Unconditional Love Belief (CULB):	→	Unconditional Love Response (ULR):	→	Unconditional Love Choice (ULC):	→	Unconditional Love Action (ULA):
I am worthy of love and acceptance as I am.		I am worthy of love and acceptance regardless of whether I have the acceptance of others.		I choose to pursue the career that I am most passionate about.		I will dedicate myself to becoming a professional pianist. I will let my parents know how I really feel and stand by my decision.

In the ULS, Curtis discovers the freedom to accept himself without needing the approval of his parents. With this freedom, he decides that he would rather pursue his passion for music than become a lawyer. Though Curtis may face some initial conflict with his parents, he is prepared for this because he realizes that he is saving himself from a lifetime of regret and inner conflict.

The next example will illustrate how it is possible to be in the ULS and still work towards the same goal. If you recall, in the CLS Rachel believed that her worthiness of love and acceptance was dependent on how successful she was in her career. This made her feel that she needed to get a promotion at work (Figure 2A). When invited to explore the ULS she discovered an entirely new way of looking at her life as depicted in Figure 2B.

Figure 2A: Rachel's Conditional Love State Addiction

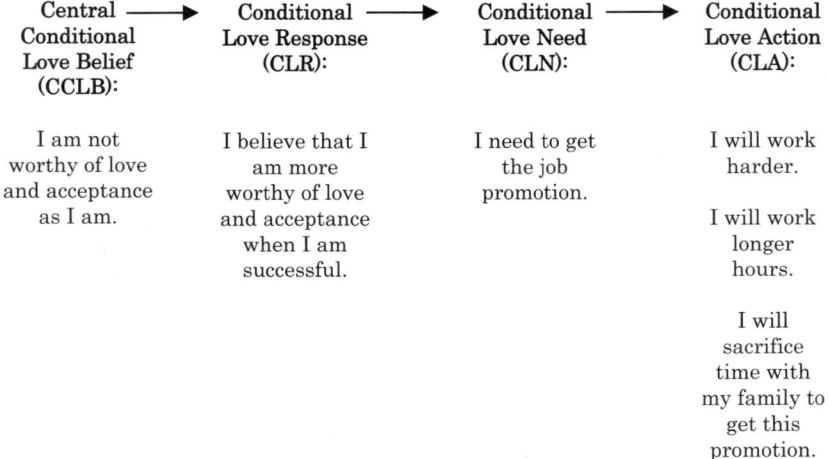

Central Conditional Love Belief (CCLB):	Conditional Love Response (CLR):	Conditional Love Need (CLN):	Conditional Love Action (CLA):
I am not worthy of love and acceptance as I am.	I believe that I am more worthy of love and acceptance when I am successful.	I need to get the job promotion.	I will work harder. I will work longer hours. I will sacrifice time with my family to get this promotion.

Figure 2B: Rachel's Behavior in the ULS

Central Unconditional Love Belief (CULB):	→ Unconditional Love Response (ULR):	→ Unconditional Love Choice (ULC):	→ Unconditional Love Action (ULA):
I am worthy of love and acceptance as I am.	I am worthy of love and acceptance regardless of whether I am successful.	I choose to pursue the job promotion because it is a great opportunity to challenge myself and develop my skills.	I will work harder. I will work longer hours while respecting my limits and my need for work-life balance.

By replacing her CCLB with the CULB, Rachel explores the possibility of no longer needing to prove her worth. This means that she no longer has to base her worthiness of acceptance on success. Notice that despite the change in her beliefs, Rachel still chooses to pursue the promotion. However, her reasons are entirely different. Her choice does not come from a need to succeed, but from a desire to challenge herself and develop new skills. On the surface, it may be difficult to observe any visible change in Rachel's behavior, but there is a change in how she feels. By changing her central belief, Rachel has opened the door to a completely different experience of life. Her esteem is no longer based on the success she achieves, and she can make choices based on the freedom that comes from knowing she is acceptable as she is. One of these choices, which was not available to her in the CLS, is to respect her limits and maintain a work-life balance.

THE FREEDOM TO CHOOSE

When you are free from the need to prove your worth, you gain the freedom to choose how you want to live. The transition from *need* to *choice* is subtle, but it makes a world of a difference on the quality of your life.

Exploring The ULS

Our deepest wishes are whispers of our authentic selves. We must learn to respect them. We must learn to listen.

SARAH BAN BREATHNACH

You will now begin your personal exploration of the ULS. It is time to look within yourself to uncover what your life could be like if you no longer needed to prove your worthiness of love and acceptance. So far you have seen how much fear and stress your addictions can cause. Now you will have the opportunity to explore what is possible when you break free from your addictions. This is a revolutionary exercise because it opens your mind to possibilities that the CLS has rendered unavailable to you. The process of exploring the ULS is deeply personal.

Take your time with this exercise because it gives you an opportunity to get in tune with yourself and determine how you want to live your life.

In this exercise, you will examine the incidents you recalled for your three major addictions and see how the central belief of the ULS can transform your experiences. To reap the full benefits of this exercise, it is important that you suspend judgment on whether or not achieving this ULS is possible or even desirable. This will only inhibit your exploration. For now, simply allow yourself to uncover how a new central belief could impact your life. This is not intended to be a purely cerebral process. Try to tap into your emotions, your feelings of what it means to be worthy of love and acceptance as you are.

Complete the following steps for each of the incidents you explored in the Breaking Down Your Addictions exercise:

1) Replace the CCLB of "I am not worthy of love and acceptance as I am" with the Central Unconditional Love Belief (CULB) of "I am worthy of love and acceptance as I am."

2) Replace the CLR pertaining to the incident with an Unconditional Love Response (ULR). To make the expression of this response easier you can begin phrasing each ULR with the following words: "I am worthy of love regardless of _____."

Fill in the blank with the words that best describe your freedom from your addiction.

3) Write down the choices (ULCs) you want to make now that you are free from your addiction. Unlike CLNs, Unconditional Love Choices are made without the need to prove anything. To help describe this choice, you can begin phrasing each ULC with the following words: "I choose to _____."

Fill in the blank with how you would choose to express your freedom in the ULS. To help you fill in this blank, imagine what choices you would make now that your CLN is no longer present.

Be especially patient with this step. Allow yourself to feel what choices unfold from this new center of freedom.

4) Describe the actions (ULAs) you want to take in order to fulfill your choices. To express these actions start with the following words: "I will_____."

For examples of this exercise, please refer to the following two pages. The examples provided are based on the same incidents described in the previous exercises.

Exploring the ULS – Example 1

Acceptance of Others Addiction (from page 116)

Central → Conditional Love Belief (CCLB):	Conditional → Love Response (CLR):	Conditional → Love Need (CLN):	Conditional Love Action (CLA):
I am not worthy of love and acceptance as I am.	I believe that I am more worthy of love and acceptance when I gain the approval of others.	I need my friends to accept and approve of me.	I will try to maintain an image of being successful at work and home so my friends will continue to admire me.

Exploration of the Unconditional Love State

Central → Unconditional Love Belief (CULB):	Unconditional → Love Response (ULR):	Unconditional → Love Choice (ULC):	Unconditional Love Action (ULA):
I am worthy of love and acceptance as I am.	I am worthy of love and acceptance regardless of whether I gain the approval of others.	I choose to have a stronger relationship with my friends so I can feel free to be myself around them.	I will stop trying to maintain a false image and share my true feelings with them including my fears, doubts and insecurities.

Exploring the ULS – Example 2

Comparison Addiction (from page 116)

Central Conditional Love Belief (CCLB):	→ Conditional Love Response (CLR):	→ Conditional Love Need (CLN):	→ Conditional Love Action (CLA):
I am not worthy of love and acceptance as I am.	I believe that I am more worthy of love and acceptance when I am better than others.	I need to be more wealthy and successful than the person I met at the party.	I will strive to achieve more. I will try to steer clear of this person so that I can avoid the feelings of insecurity that he evokes in me.

Exploration of the Unconditional Love State

Central Unconditional Love Belief (CULB):	→ Unconditional Love Response (ULR):	→ Unconditional Love Choice (ULC):	→ Unconditional Love Action (ULA):
I am worthy of love and acceptance as I am.	I am worthy of love and acceptance regardless of how I compare to others.	I choose to stay content with my current job, and spend my time on things that are more important to me.	I will continue working hard at my job. I will spend my spare time enjoying my hobbies, and being with the people who are close to me.

SOME COMMONLY ASKED QUESTIONS

If I don't need a reason to feel worthy of love, what would be my motivation for doing anything?

In the CLS the primary motivation for doing anything is fear. Although fear is a powerful motivator it is not the only one, and it is usually more damaging than effective. Often, our fear can cloud our mind and drain our creative energy. Fear can arise from every CLS Addiction because the moment we impose conditions on our self-worth, we grow fearful of not fulfilling those conditions.

Most of us have become so accustomed to being motivated by fear that it is hard to fathom being driven by anything else. Since the fear that is produced by our addictions motivates so many of our actions, some people worry that if they start to accept themselves as they are, they will lose the motivation to do anything. This is a misconception based on the idea that we can only be motivated by fear. Simple observation can dispel this myth. For example, there are times when people stand up for something they believe in even if they are afraid of the consequences. Under such circumstances, something else is motivating them. When we do the things we really enjoy, fear is not motivating us, but we are still driven to act. When we express our love to others, something other than fear is usually motivating us.

By exploring the ULS, you give yourself the rare opportunity to put aside your fear and tap into your deeper motivations in life. You have already started this process in the previous exercise of Exploring the ULS. Look back to the choices you made and notice that each one was made in the absence of fear. Consider what your motivation was when you made these choices. What you uncover will help point the way to new sources of motivation.

If I no longer seek the acceptance of others, I foresee that some of my family or friends will disapprove of my new behavior. Enjoying their love is important to me. Are you saying that I should give up these relationships?

Feeling worthy of love and acceptance does not prevent you from valuing relationships. In fact, when you no longer need the love of others, you will be freer to enjoy the love they offer without imposing your demands on them. Such love is without the expectations that so often damage relationships and prevent us from appreciating each other. In this way, the ULS enriches relationships.

That being said, it is still entirely possible that some people in your life will not appreciate your new behavior. You may even lose some friendships when you decide to be true to yourself. This raises an important question: Were these people really your friends, or were they just friends to the impression they had of you? Anytime someone requires you to conform to their expectations, you are not engaging in a healthy relationship. People who demand that you remain a certain way are less concerned about you and more concerned about maintaining their image of you. But, you are not a static image. You are a dynamic being capable of continuous growth and expansion. When people refuse to accept this, they inhibit you and prevent your relationship with them from evolving.

If you happen to lose some friendships along the way, your journey to freedom will more than compensate for this loss. It will open the door to stronger connections and more honesty with the friends that remain, and any new friends you attract into your life. More importantly, the relationship you build with yourself in the ULS will allow you to tap into an abundant source of self-love and support. This love from within is much more powerful than anything you could find outside of yourself.

Isn't it human nature to feel that we need to prove our worthiness of love?

If it was human nature to prove our worthiness of love and acceptance, that would imply that it is beyond our capacity to change. When we come to such a conclusion, we undermine our power to transform our lives. It is easy to make this mistake because we often confuse "our nature" with what seems to be natural due to our conditioning. The CLS seems natural because we have never known any other way of experiencing love and acceptance. However, the idea that we need to prove our worthiness of love is nothing more than a belief. And like any belief, it can be challenged and changed.

Now that you have been introduced to the Unconditional Love State, you understand that a very real alternative exists. Your new awareness puts you in an exceptional position. It empowers you to challenge the ideas that you may have taken for granted, and choose your own "nature."

CONSTITUTIONAL FREEDOM IS NOT ENOUGH

In democratic nations, citizens are entitled to the fundamental freedom of thought, opinion and expression. Yet, how can anyone exercise such freedom, in its true sense, if we are conditioned to fear the judgments of others? Most of us do what is expected of us because we fear the disapproval and condemnation that may arise from challenging the status quo. We face tremendous pressure from all sides. In "free" societies this pressure is very subtle. The expectations of our family, friends, school, religion, job, and culture put pressure upon us to conform. Such conformity breeds uniformity of thought.

Of course, a certain amount of cooperation is necessary for any society to function and to avoid anarchy; however, uniformity of thought deprives our civilization of new ideas and perspectives necessary for its evolution. Creativity is born in environments where people are free to challenge all that might be taken for granted. Consequently, no society can continue to evolve in a positive direction when a culture of fear pervades the hearts and minds of its people.

The fear of what others think deprives most citizens of democratic nations from ever realizing the fundamental freedoms their constitution legally grants them. As long as there is this fear, you cannot have freedom of thought and expression. Constitutional freedom is only the beginning. To truly reclaim our personal and social freedoms we must challenge our need for the acceptance of others.

WEIGHING YOUR OPTIONS

In the previous exercise, you explored the possibility of replacing the central belief of the CLS with the central belief of the ULS. Now you will pursue this analysis further by comparing these two options.

> **To complete this exercise you will assess the advantages and disadvantages of each state for the incidents you have been examining.**

Weighing Your Options requires an honest analysis of the CLS and ULS. The reality is that there are advantages and disadvantages to both of these states. This crucial evaluation will help you assess the consequences of these two distinct ways of living. The more thorough your investigation, the better you will be at determining the possibilities each state has to offer you. Your analysis will allow you to further assess how each of these states can affect you differently. Only by taking the time to do this exercise can you make a meaningful decision as to which central belief you wish to adopt. In addition, this process will give you the clarity and resolve to follow through on whichever decision you eventually make.

For examples of this exercise, please refer to the following two pages. The examples provided are based on the same incidents described in the previous exercises.

WEIGHING YOUR OPTIONS – EXAMPLE 1

UAcceptance of Others Addiction → Behavior in the ULS

(CLN): I need my friends to accept and approve of me.

(CLA): I will try to maintain an image of being successful at work and home so my friends will continue to admire me.

(ULC): I choose to have a stronger relationship with my friends so I can feel free to be myself around them.

(ULA): I will stop trying to maintain a false image and share my true feelings with them including my fears, doubts, & insecurities.

ADVANTAGES	DISADVANTAGES
- I like the feeling of knowing that my friends admire and respect me. - I feel appreciated and validated.	- The validation I do feel is short-lived. - Maintaining an image of being successful, especially when I feel down, is very difficult. It can also be tiring. - I suppress my emotions and have no one to share my true thoughts and feelings with. - I do not feel free to be myself.

ADVANTAGES	DISADVANTAGES
- I will have the freedom to feel good about myself regardless of whether my friends respect me. - I will alleviate the stress of trying to maintain an image of being successful at all times. - By sharing my real feelings I will strengthen our friendship. Whatever connections we do have will become more authentic.	- I must make the effort of no longer relying on the need for my friends' approval and this may be difficult at first. - Initially, it will be difficult to reveal my fears and insecurities with my friends.

WEIGHING YOUR OPTIONS – EXAMPLE 2

Comparison Addiction

Behavior in the ULS

(CLN):
I need to be more wealthy and successful than the person I met at the party.

(CLA):
I will strive to achieve more. I will try to steer clear of this person so that I can avoid the feelings of insecurity that he evokes in me.

(ULC):
I choose to stay content with my current job and spend my time on things that are more important to me.

(ULA):
I will continue working hard at my job. I will spend my spare time enjoying hobbies and being with people who are close to me.

ADVANTAGES	DISADVANTAGES
- I feel better about myself when I am around those who have achieved less than me. - When I compare myself with other people it can motivate me to achieve more. - When I am more successful, other people give me more attention and care more about what I have to say.	- By comparing myself to others, I base my self-worth on things I cannot control. - I find it stressful to keep up with those I compare myself with. - I dislike feeling insecure about myself & jealous of others. - I can lose track of what is most important to me while trying to compete with others.

ADVANTAGES	DISADVANTAGES
- I can enjoy the freedom of not basing my self-worth on how I compare with others. - I can do what I really want without the pressure of needing to prove my worth. - I can appreciate the achievements of others without feeling threatened by them. I may even seek to learn from them.	- It will take time to break free from the habit of comparing myself with others. - I may no longer be motivated to do the things that other people approve of. This may result in losing the praise and esteem of others.

Making the Choice

Everything can be taken from a man but the last of human freedoms, the right to choose one's attitude in any given set of circumstances – the right to choose one's own way.

Viktor Frankl

The Women's Liberation movement is a perfect example of how a central belief can change despite years of social conditioning. It also sets a precedent for the type of change you have begun to explore in the ULS.

However, there is a major difference between these situations. During the Women's Liberation movement, there were distinct laws that prevented women from realizing their freedom of equality in everyday life. For example, they were prevented by law from voting. To enjoy the freedom of equality, it was not enough for women to believe that they were equal. To experience freedom in their lives, a social revolution was required.

Fortunately, there are no laws that prevent you from accepting yourself. This means that the freedom of the ULS is available to you right now. If you choose to accept yourself as you are, no one can stop you. People may judge you, but they cannot take away your self-love or self-acceptance without your consent. If you want to stop investing time and energy in your addictions, you can do it. If you want to stop being hard on yourself, you can do it. If you want to start moving towards goals without basing your worth on the results, you can. That is the beauty of the exploration that you have begun. For the most part, the freedom you will discover in the ULS is accessible to you at each and every moment... if you choose.

Your power of choice is the first crucial step to changing your central beliefs, and this power is completely in your hands. Make no mistake about it. Deciding between the CCLB and the CULB is entirely a matter of choice. Neither belief can be proved or disproved. Central beliefs are special in this sense because they are the building blocks of your life philosophy. They form the starting point of how your life will unfold, but they are not proven. They are chosen.

Once you understand this, you will empower yourself with a wisdom that can transform your life.

> **Central beliefs are chosen. Either you consciously choose them or they are chosen for you through conditioning.**

You can choose to believe that you are worthy of love as you are, or you can choose to believe that you are not. Each belief is just as valid as the other. Yet, each of them inspires completely different life experiences. The CLS is familiar, but is also the source of your stress, fears, and insecurities. You can choose the central belief of the CLS and stay stuck in the web of your addictions, always trying to prove your worthiness of love. Or you can choose the central belief of the ULS and let yourself experience that love and acceptance right now.

With your new awareness, this choice is now entirely yours. It is a matter of choosing between two central beliefs, and only you can make this decision. **What will you choose?**

When Is Enough, Enough?

For people with substance addictions, positive changes often occur only after living with the addiction and watching it destroy the things they hold dear to them such as their family, friends and career. There can come a time in an addict's life when he or she finally says "enough is enough." When this happens, it is a critical turning point. This is when the addict resolves to move beyond his or her addiction. This one decision can dramatically change the course of the addict's life.

All your life, you have endured the emotional pain and limitations of your CLS Addictions. Having reached this far along the Born on the Mountaintop journey, you have also seen how the CLS destroys the possibility of feeling worthy of love as you are. Yet, it does not have to be this way. You do not have to live in the CLS anymore. That is the boon of the ULS. If you choose, you can accept yourself as you are right now, and free yourself from the grip of your addictions. You have reached the crossroads of this journey where you are empowered to choose between these two states. How long will you search for fulfillment where it cannot be found? How much longer will you live without realizing freedom from the fears and insecurities that stop you from feeling truly alive? Have you reached that turning point in your life where enough is enough?

The Journey Ahead

If we lived in a world that reinforced the idea that we do not have to prove our worth, making the choice to move towards the ULS would be sufficient to reclaim our personal freedom. We would simply make the choice and the encouragement from our environment would propel us towards our freedom. We have seen, however, that we live in a very different world, one that is constantly reinforcing the CLS. Not only that, these messages of conditional love have been internalized and manifest themselves in our lives as addictions. The result is that we habitually concern ourselves with proving our worth and feel bad whenever we cannot. The combination of these external and internal pressures makes the pull towards the CLS very strong. It can also make us overlook our immense power to choose what we believe about ourselves.

The ULS is a revolutionary way of perceiving ourselves and the world. By choosing to believe that we are worthy of love and acceptance as we are, we are defying years of social conditioning at the deepest level. The ramifications of this choice can affect every aspect of our lives including how we think, feel, and act. That is why those who have chosen the ULS require a strategy to help break free from the CLS and integrate this choice into their lives. The remaining sections of the book focus on providing you with tools and exercises towards this end. As you go through the remainder of the journey, you will also further explore how the freedom of the ULS can change your life.

There are three remaining sections in this book: Mind Transformation, Manifestation, and Keeping the Commitment. Mind Transformation focuses on integrating the ULS into the way you think and feel. Manifestation introduces techniques to affirm the ULS in your day-to-day activities. This also involves exploring how you can act in ways that let others know that they, too, are worthy of love as they are. In the Keeping the Commitment section you will explore tools that will help you honor the commitments you have made to yourself. Together, these remaining stages of the journey form a holistic approach of integrating the ULS into your life.

Important Things to Remember Before Resuming Your Journey:

1. While exploring the tools in the remaining sections of the book, keep in mind that you are not expected to apply all of them immediately. After you have tried using all the tools once, we will give you further guidance on how to gradually integrate them into your life.

2. As you incorporate the ULS into your life, be careful to avoid the tendency of basing your worth on achieving this goal. Such an idea contradicts the entire spirit of the ULS because it creates another condition on your self-worth. This subject is so important that we have devoted an entire section to it towards the end of the book.

PART 2

MIND TRANSFORMATION

RESHAPING YOUR BELIEFS

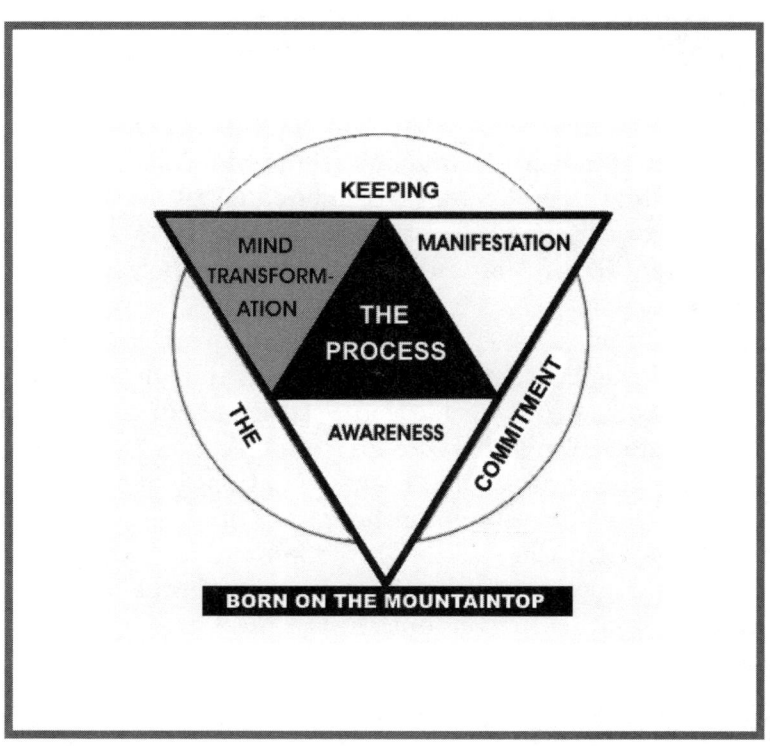

MIND TRANSFORMATION

*Emancipate yourselves from mental slavery;
None but ourselves can free our minds.*

BOB MARLEY

When we come across a tree in the woods, we may notice its trunk, leaves, and branches. These are the most visible and obvious features of the tree. Yet, we all know that there is an entire world of activity occurring beneath the surface. The tree's roots extend deep into the ground drawing nutrients from the soil, and its leaves release oxygen into the air. All of these activities have an impact on the tree's well-being even though we cannot see them. You are no different in this regard. Beneath the surface of your actions is a world of activity that cannot be seen and that is all taking place within your mind. Your invisible thoughts and feelings motivate you to act and have a tremendous influence on your experience of life. In fact, even as you read these words, your present mental state is affecting the quality of your reading experience.

As you embark on your exploration of the ULS, it is important to concentrate on transforming your mind. For it is here, in this invisible world, that you can begin to plant new thoughts and feelings that honor your decision to be worthy of love as you are. Mind Transformation is a systematic process of transforming your thoughts and emotions so that they align with the ULS. Throughout this phase of the journey you will experiment with numerous tools and techniques that help you uproot the CLS and nurture the central belief of the ULS.

What separates the CLS from the ULS is essentially a single central belief. The difference in this central belief results in radically different ways of perceiving the world and living life. You have already examined the addictions that arise from the central belief of the CLS. Despite how influential these addictions can be, they exist solely in your mind and are composed of interrelated thoughts, images, and memories. Fortunately, each of these elements can be challenged and replaced to give birth to a new mind in harmony with your choice to be worthy of love as you are. This new mind will inevitably express itself through a new life, a life that is free from the chains of the mind and heart. To break the web of your addictions, you need to explore ways of challenging the old ideas you have about yourself. Mind Transformation will reveal how to replace the central belief of the CLS with the central belief of the ULS, so that you can realize the peace of mind that comes from completely accepting yourself.

Principles of the Mind

The greatest discovery of our generation is that human beings can alter their lives by altering their attitudes of mind. As you think, so shall you be.

William James

Before we officially begin your introduction to the Mind Transformation tools, it is important that we touch upon some fundamental principles of the mind. These timeless principles have been incorporated into the development and application of many of the tools to follow.

1. What you resist, persists.

These words were said by Carl Jung and summarize an important principle of the mind. When moving towards personal transformation, usually our first response is to condemn that which we want to change about ourselves. However, by doing this, we not only engage in unhealthy denial and repression of our emotions, we also end up strengthening these emotions within our psyches. At the same time, the internal conflict created prevents us from being aware of what is truly happening. To avoid this ineffective approach, the Mind Transformation tools first work to establish an attitude of complete acceptance of your current state, so that you may enjoy a peaceful approach to implementing change in your life.

2. You are what you think you are.

This is a fundamental law of the mind. As you think, so shall you be. You have thousands of thoughts each day. Most of them belong to mental patterns that have been conditioned into your psyche for years. Almost every thought you have makes an impact on your perception and your mood. The principle of understanding your current thoughts and using new thoughts to create the life you want is an integral feature of the Mind Transformation tools.

3. You are what you imagine yourself to be.

You articulate yourself with words, but you think in images. Simply imagining a happy time in your life or a beautiful landscape can immediately transform your emotional state. You will come to appreciate how using the power of visualization to your advantage can help make a substantial impact on how you feel and approach life.

4. Your mind responds best to emotion.

Whatever thoughts or visualizations you endow with emotion, whether positive or negative, are the ones that most influence your state of being. While applying the tools to follow, this principle can be used to your advantage by consciously charging your thoughts and visualizations with positive emotions. If this is not done, the potential benefits you can realize from these tools will be compromised.

When using the principles of the mind, remember that these are principles you are already using all the time! Your thoughts, visual perceptions, and emotions are impacting you at nearly every moment whether you realize it or not. You can either use these principles to your advantage, or have them continue to influence you to your disadvantage.

Do not underestimate how powerful these principles of the mind are. They are already being used by people from all walks-of-life to accomplish extraordinary feats. Since the tools to come incorporate these principles, experimenting with them is like experimenting with the controls of your life. The consistent application of these tools will allow you to steer your life towards the freedom of the ULS. We encourage you to enjoy this process. Play with the tools and discover just how much of your life has always been in your hands.

THE TOOLS

The Mind Transformation tools have been divided into the following three sections:

1) You will begin with the Awareness Journal, a tool that will allow you to build your awareness of how the CLS and ULS are affecting you. It also empowers you to recognize opportunities for integrating the ULS into your life. Keeping an Awareness Journal encourages daily reflection on how your thoughts and emotions impact your experiences and how you can change them to break free from inhibiting patterns.

2) With the help of the next two tools you will focus on letting go of the hold the CLS has on your life:

(i) A Letter to Your CLS

When most people attempt to make personal changes, they usually face some internal conflict. This conflict often arises from approaching personal change in a harsh and disrespectful manner. A Letter to Your CLS is a tool that helps you to avoid creating such conflict in your life as you move towards the ULS.

(ii) Releasing the Past

You have lived most of your life with your CLS Addictions. Despite having made the decision to free yourself from these addictions, the harmful impact these addictions have had on your life still remains. Releasing the Past is a powerful tool that helps you address and release the hurt that has built up within you over the years.

Both of these tools focus on making peace with the CLS. They help you let go of the CLS that has been a major part of your life for so many years and make way for the freedom of the ULS.

3) The next set of tools focus on building a new foundation of the ULS within your mind and heart.

(i) Tapping into the ULS

To appreciate the significance of the ULS, you must experience what it really feels like to completely love and accept yourself as you are. By learning the simple steps of Tapping into the ULS, you will be able to access this part of yourself at any time.

(ii) Mind Scripting

You are what you think you are. This principle of the mind is the essence of the Mind Scripting tool. All your life, your mind has been fed a regular diet of thoughts that reflect the CLS. If you want to change your life, you must change your mental diet. Mind Scripting empowers you with an effective strategy to make such a change possible.

(iii) Lucid Living

You are what you imagine yourself to be. Deep inside your subconscious is a visual blueprint of who you think you are. Much of your behavior and personality are manifestations of this internal vision. To reclaim the freedom to be who you choose, you must actively feed your mind new visualizations related to the ULS. Lucid Living will show you an effective way of making this transformation possible.

(iv) D-Mapping

D-Mapping uses the power of thoughts and visual imagery to reinforce the ULS in your life. While creating your D-Map you will explore the positive emotions, thoughts and visions that the ULS inspires in you and use this knowledge to further transform your life.

THE SUBCONSCIOUS MIND:

"...our brains become magnetized with the dominating thoughts which we hold in our minds, and, by means with which no man is familiar, these 'magnets' attract to us the forces, the people, the circumstances of life which harmonize with the nature of our dominating thoughts." -Napoleon Hill

For ages, people have been using the powers of their subconscious mind to alter their attitudes or attract what they want into their lives. Whether it be through the Law of Attraction that Napoleon Hill describes above, visualization, hypnotic suggestion, or other tools, the power of the subconscious mind is usually taught to help people get what they want from life. Consequently, most people use their subconscious mind for purposes such as losing weight or feeling calm, or attracting success, wealth, relationships and whatever else they desire.

But, if you believe you need to prove your worth, no matter how much you change your attitude or what you attract into your life, a true sense of fulfillment will always elude you. If you do not first resolve your addictions, you will end up using the subconscious mind to perpetuate them, and this will only push you further along a never-ending journey to prove your worth.

Many of the Mind Transformation tools work on the conscious and subconscious level. What makes them especially ingenious is that they apply the power of the subconscious mind to give you the fulfillment of knowing that you are worthy of love as you are – a fulfillment without rules or conditions and free from the slavery of your addictions.

The Awareness Journal

Great news! The exercises you have completed in the Awareness section have already contributed to transforming the way you perceive yourself and the world. Now that you are aware of your addictions and the ULS, your life cannot be the same. The natural and almost effortless change that awareness facilitates makes it one of the greatest sources of personal transformation. By simply watching yourself without prejudice you can drill to the heart of what is really happening inside you.

Your awareness of the ULS and CLS does not stop with the exercises you have done so far. In fact, you are just beginning to discover how powerful a force awareness can be towards reclaiming your freedom. The ULS represents a very different approach with far-reaching implications. If you are serious about breaking free from addictions, then you have to take the time to understand what is driving your thoughts and behaviors.

Also understanding how you can incorporate the freedom of the ULS into your life will take patience and regular reflection. You have to start asking yourself: What would you want if you were free, and how can you make that freedom a reality? The answers you uncover will be unique because you are a unique person with your own set of circumstances.

It is important to respect that all the answers you are looking for are within you. As your understanding of yourself gets clearer, the answers you are looking for will arrive. All you have to do is keep asking the right questions, and the answers will pop into your head as if they were waiting for you all along. That is where the Awareness Journal comes in.

The Awareness Journal is the most effective tool for building your awareness and discovering practical ways of realizing the freedom of the ULS in your life. It is easy to use and only requires about fifteen minutes of your time. To apply the tool, all you need to do is reflect on the day's events without judgment and answer the following questions:

1) How has the CLS affected me today?

Your addictions are likely affecting you in different ways each day. Answer this question by describing the major ways in which your addictions have affected you today. By answering this question you will expand your awareness of the role that the CLS plays in your life.

2) How has the ULS affected me today?

Since you will be doing regular exercises to help reclaim your personal freedom, it is encouraging to have a record of the ways in which these exercises impact your life. For this question, describe the ways in which the new central belief of the ULS has affected you today.

3) In the instances where the CLS affected me, how would I choose to act differently knowing that I am worthy of love as I am?

This question allows for a deeper exploration of the ULS and the choices you want to make. To discover new options, you may find it helpful to follow the steps outlined in the Exploring the ULS exercise.

4) How can I make these choices a reality when similar incidences occur?

This final question encourages you to find practical ways of integrating your choices into your life.

Asking the right questions allows you to learn so much about yourself. Taking just fifteen minutes to answer the four questions above will help clarify your thoughts and deepen your understanding of who you are and what you can become. The Awareness Journal is a powerful ally in helping you recognize the impact of your addictions. Most importantly, it will help you develop your own way of expressing the many freedoms of the ULS.

STEPPING INTO REALITY

What do you do when you have a bad headache? Most of us reach for an Aspirin or Tylenol to give us some relief. In the midst of pain and discomfort, this reaction seems logical. The headache, however, is merely a symptom of a deeper problem. It could be the symptom of illness, stress, poor diet or a combination thereof. Though headache medication may provide some temporary relief, it does not deal with the root cause of the pain.

Similarly, much of what we struggle with, whether it be our hurt, fear, anger, stress or dissatisfaction, are symptoms of a much deeper problem related to the central belief of the CLS. In dealing with these issues we have a similar choice to make – we can choose between temporary relief or lasting solutions. Despite the best of intentions, many of us end up seeking temporary relief. Sometimes this happens due to our impatience. After all, securing lasting solutions takes more work and dedication. Yet, often we are just misled. There are too many people out there selling quick fixes – a magic pill that will solve all our problems. But, there is no such magic pill. A lifetime of conditioning is not overcome in a day. To transform your experience of life at a deepest level takes patience and commitment. It is a very personal process.

Awareness is all about facing ourselves. It entails looking within to see what is happening and uncovering new possibilities. To do this, we must refrain from rushing to find an answer because this clouds our ability to see what is really going on. To see with complete awareness, it is important to leave all our preconceived notions behind because these notions filter reality.

Awareness takes courage, the guts to step into reality. Only then can we stare into the problem with the calm, unflinching eye of an objective observer and uncover a lasting solution. Are you ready? It's time to face yourself and step into it!

A Letter To Your CLS

When I let go of what I am, I become what I might be.
LAO TZU

We now move on to making peace with the CLS. In other words, making peace with that part of our psyche that habitually demands proof of our self-worth. While making a change, one of the most common mistakes we can make is condemning that part of ourselves we wish to change. By labeling the CLS as either something "wrong" or "bad," we set ourselves up to wage an internal battle with ourselves. As a result, we can feel guilty or frustrated whenever our addictions arise. Such an approach can be very destructive to our self-worth because the CLS is such a big part of our lives. Clearly, it is in our best interest to avoid this common tendency right from the start.

The purpose of this exercise is to let go of the CLS in a spirit of compassion by writing a letter to your CLS. You will acknowledge your appreciation for all that your CLS has been trying to achieve for you in this letter. This may seem puzzling. You may wonder, why you are being asked to express appreciation for something that is limiting your freedom. Though the inhibiting nature of your CLS is now clear to you, you previously relied on it to feel love in your life. Up until now, you were aware of no other alternative. Your addictions have been trying to help you feel love in the only way you knew how. To condemn this innocent behavior on your part is unfair and hurtful. That is why appreciating the original intent of the CLS is a crucial part of this letter and should be kept in mind whenever your addictions arise in the future.

After acknowledging the role the CLS has played, describe how the CLS is inhibiting you from living the life you want. Then explain why you want to replace it with the ULS. To help you articulate these thoughts you may choose to draw from the work you have already done in the Weighing Your Options exercise.

As in all exercises of this book, A Letter to your CLS is not

MIND TRANSFORMATION

meant to be a purely cerebral process. You are encouraged to take the time to get in touch with your emotions as you write to this part of your psyche. When you do, you will find that the letter can be a therapeutic process. Writing this letter will save you from all the guilt and frustration that can come from condemning the CLS. By completing this peace contract with yourself, you will assure a smooth and joyful transition into the ULS.

Here is a breakdown of a possible way to structure your letter:

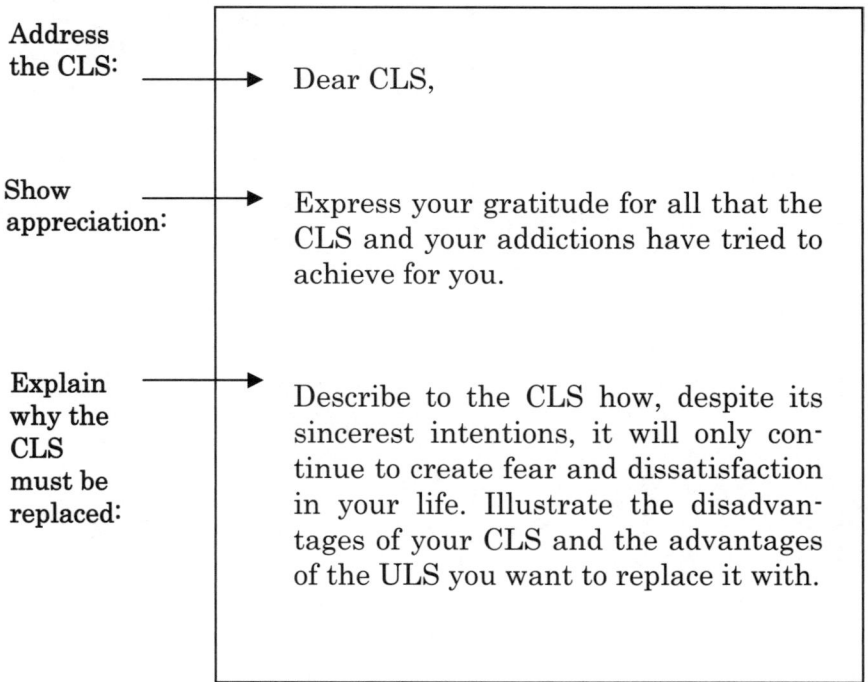

Address the CLS: → Dear CLS,

Show appreciation: → Express your gratitude for all that the CLS and your addictions have tried to achieve for you.

Explain why the CLS must be replaced: → Describe to the CLS how, despite its sincerest intentions, it will only continue to create fear and dissatisfaction in your life. Illustrate the disadvantages of your CLS and the advantages of the ULS you want to replace it with.

> ## The Verdict Is In
>
> While writing your letter to the CLS, you may discover that the CLS has played a distinct role in your life. For example, a student of the Born on the Mountaintop course realized that her relationship to the CLS was similar to that of a defendant and her lawyer. She felt like she was the defendant and her CLS was her lawyer constantly presenting a case for her worthiness of love. She was able to dismiss her inner lawyer after realizing that the ULS no longer required her to prove her worth. The verdict was in – she was already worthy of love.

Releasing The Past

The old skin has to be shed before the new one can come.

JOSEPH CAMPBELL

Though we cannot live in the past, many of us let our past live inside us. Unable to understand or cope with painful experiences in our lives, we tend to suppress our emotions. Sometimes these repressed feelings manifest as physical ailments in our body. Other times they create mental blocks that stifle our ability to creatively deal with life's challenges. These emotions will not disappear until we learn to acknowledge, accept and understand them.

How would you feel if you were in a relationship with someone who could not accept you for who you are and constantly criticized your faults? Most of us would feel uncomfortable around such people because of the constant fear of doing something that might upset them. Yet, you have often been in a similar type of relationship with yourself. Your CLS Addictions have prevented you from accepting yourself as you are. This has kept you in fear of not being able to prove yourself worthy of the acceptance you long for. Whenever you were unable to meet the conditions you placed on your self-worth, you experienced the pain of not being acceptable. Every time you sought to prove your worth through fulfilling your addictions, you were simultaneously communicating to yourself the painful message that you were not good enough. You have been carrying the hurt from these painful messages all your life. Until you find a constructive way of addressing this pain, it shall remain suppressed inside you.

In this exercise you will be asked to look back on your past and recall events where you gave yourself the message that you are not worthy of love as you are. You will then be asking yourself for forgiveness regarding the hurt you have inflicted on yourself with this message.

> For the purposes of this exercise, a transgression is any of your past thoughts or actions that have reinforced the message that you are not worthy of love as you are.

This exercise involves the completion of the following steps:

1) Reflecting on your past

Find somewhere quiet to reflect on your life and identify the significant transgressions towards yourself. It would be impossible to account for each one since most of us commit many transgressions every day. For the purposes of this exercise, you need to focus on the key events of your life. You might recall your failures, embarrassing moments, trials and tribulations. You might even remember your fond memories and achievements as they may have also been instances when you reinforced the message that you could only feel better about yourself when you proved that you were worthy of this feeling.

2) Apologizing to yourself

Once you have listed your transgressions, schedule a block of uninterrupted time dedicated to asking forgiveness from yourself for each one. Be sure to find a secluded place where you can have a free and candid, heart-to-heart discussion with yourself. Try to imagine the event as it occurred, and apologize to yourself.

Some people argue against apologizing for something that they did not intentionally do. However, the intention of this exercise is not to make you feel guilty about the past, nor to place blame on you for the conditioning that has shaped your CLS. Instead, this Releasing the Past exercise helps you utilize the principle of forgiveness to release suppressed emotions inside you. Asking forgiveness allows you to heal yourself from the consequences of your behavior in the past, regardless of whether you were conscious of it or not. When you engage in the courageous act of apologizing, you also strengthen your resolve to love unconditionally in the future.

3) Sharing (optional)

After asking forgiveness from yourself, you have the option of sharing the transgressions you made against yourself. Since this entails disclosing very personal information, it is important that you find someone in whom you can totally confide. Moreover, the person you select should be someone you can trust to be supportive of your efforts.

This person's role is to simply listen without judgment and with a genuine desire to understand. Describe to him/her the circumstances surrounding each transgression. Explain how each transgression is a manifestation of a CLS Addiction that you have. If you are able to find someone with whom you can share your transgressions, you will allow for greater emotional release. Also, by admitting the pain you have caused yourself to another, you fortify your commitment to change in the future.

Releasing the Past is an essential step to healing yourself. When you let go of all your hurt, you unload the heavy burden of your addictive past. Each apology takes you closer and closer to realizing the emotional freedom of accepting and being yourself.

For an example of this exercise, please refer to the next page.

Please note that if some of the events in your past are too painful to recall or if this exercise becomes too intense, we recommend that you do not vividly recall those particular events at this time. You may not be ready to release this part of your past, or may require some professional help to resolve these issues. The purpose of this exercise is to let go of the pain in a peaceful manner, *not* to cause further emotional trauma.

Releasing The Past – Example

Age	Circumstance	Transgressions To Self
12	<u>Acceptance of Others</u>: The first time I came home after failing a test, I was very afraid of how disappointed my parents might be.	I can still remember the look on my father's face that day. He was so disappointed in me. I felt like a total failure. From then on, I tried to avoid receiving that look again. To this day, whenever I receive that look from him, I feel awful about myself. I find it hard to accept myself knowing he is unhappy with me.
18	<u>"The One"</u>: I fell in love with a boy from high school. When I approached him to go on a date he refused.	I was devastated. The rejection shattered my heart. I could not find myself worthy of love knowing the person I was attracted to did not find me worthy of his love.
27	<u>Acceptance of Others</u>: At work I was so concerned about what my colleagues thought of me that I did not feel comfortable being myself.	I was so afraid that people would not accept me that I never opened up. I only talked about things that I knew other people would find agreeable. By doing this, I was indirectly telling myself that I was not acceptable unless my colleagues thought I was acceptable.
45	<u>Appearance</u>: As I started to notice more and more wrinkles and white hairs, I began to panic. I became very concerned about looking old in the eyes of other people. I knew that if people stopped giving me the attention they used to, I would feel less beautiful inside. To compensate, I spent more time putting make-up on and dying my hair.	I felt less acceptable because I knew that people would find me less attractive. I spent a lot of time putting make-up on every day because I could not feel worthy of love knowing I looked old.

TAPPING INTO THE ULS

The astounding significance of the ULS can only be understood by those who experience it with all their senses. Tapping into the ULS is all about making this experience known to you. This tool is designed to empower you to feel unconditional love whenever you choose. It also allows you to get in tune with yourself and further investigate what the freedom of the ULS signifies in your life.

Before learning how to tap into the ULS, we must explore a phenomenon called the *Floodgates of Love*. This phenomenon provides a significant insight into how the CLS is inhibiting your life and how drastically different the ULS is.

The Floodgates of Love

Floodgates are essentially walls that block the flow of flooding water. When they are closed the water's movement is stopped, and when they are opened the water is able to flow. The way floodgates function is remarkably similar to how the CLS allows you to experience love in your life. Think of the water as the love and acceptance you seek. The gates themselves are the conditions you place on your ability to experience that love. In other words, whenever you fulfill your conditions you open the gates and let yourself feel love and acceptance. When you do not fulfill your conditions, you close the gates and cannot feel love until you, once again, prove yourself worthy of it. These are the Floodgates of Love.

The important thing to recognize is that you are always controlling the gates. Furthermore, the love and acceptance you seek through your addictions is always available to you. It is always there! But, you do not allow yourself to feel it until you fulfill your conditions.

The ULS completely challenges the Floodgates of Love. It shows you that you do not need to place conditions on the flow of love and allows you to experience love with no conditions whatsoever.

The purpose of Tapping Into The ULS is to give yourself permission, for at least 5 minutes a day, to open the

Floodgates of Love so that you may feel what it means to love yourself without conditions. Here are the simple steps to this exercise:

1) Tapping in

i) While applying this tool, you may lie down and close your eyes to help enhance your focus. Relax while taking a few deep breaths. With every exhalation let yourself relax more and more. Take a moment to release the tension from each part of your body.

ii) Calmly and assuredly say to yourself "I choose to believe that I am worthy of love as I am." This is a powerful way of opening the Floodgates of Love and accessing the ULS because it reminds you that the ULS is a choice.

iii) Now, one by one, let go of each of your addictions. Let go of the need to become or achieve anything for this brief period. Let yourself accept whatever you may be feeling in this moment. Remember, there is nothing more to prove. Even let go of the need to do this exercise well. Immerse yourself in the realization that you are worthy of love as you are.

2) Float in the feeling

After you let go of the need to be or do anything, let yourself float in this feeling. Simply relax and see where it takes you.

3) Investigate (optional)

This exercise presents the exciting opportunity to tap into an entirely unique perspective. Once you have taken the time to float in the feeling, you can take advantage of this state by exploring what new possibilities arise from the ULS. You may do this by asking yourself questions. For example, you may ask: How am I feeling right now? What do I want to do today? or What do I want in my life? Truly, there is no limit to what you can investigate in this state of being.

Your answers may come to you in the form of words, images or something entirely different. At times, you may be surprised by what is revealed. You do not always have to follow what you discover, but you should respect the thoughts and feelings that do arise. They come from a sacred place within yourself, a place that is not afraid and longs for freedom.

While you explore, try not to let your thoughts of what is possible interfere with your investigation. Too often what is possible has been defined and limited by the CLS. That's the fun of this exercise. No one can tell you what you will uncover because this is your inner world. Exploring where your freedom will take you is the gift of this exercise. Enjoy it.

Relax & Uncover

The method of Tapping into the ULS presented above is a suggestion. In reality, there are as many ways to tap into the ULS as there are people. At the very least, we recommend that you begin the exercise by relaxing your body in some way, and saying the words "I choose to be worthy of love as I am." After this, we encourage you to experiment with your own way of Tapping into the ULS. Some people play music in the background, some sing songs to themselves, some even imagine people they love and direct those feelings of love to themselves. The essential point is to let yourself experience love without conditions. How you do this, is up to you.

If you experience some resistance while doing this exercise, it is perfectly natural. Try not to force yourself to feel anything, because there is absolutely no ideal to strive for. You are worthy of acceptance as you are. Simply give yourself permission to experiment with this state for a few minutes each day. The more time you spend exploring this state, the more you are bound to uncover.

Mind Scripting

It is amazing how an actor can convince you that he is Romeo in one moment and Caesar in the next. Just as an actor's role is defined by a script, your role in this drama of life is defined by a script as well, a script composed of the thoughts that exist in your mind. The key to transforming your life lies in changing your thoughts, for they define who you are. Mind Scripting teaches you how to write your own script. You will learn to replace the old scripts of your CLS Addictions with new scripts that declare your freedom to love and accept yourself as you are. This will empower you to become the author of your own destiny.

Often people find it strange to come across someone who is talking to himself aloud. However, the truth is we all talk to ourselves. Only most of us do so silently in our minds. An important question to ask yourself is: What do you say when you talk to yourself? After all, what you say is influencing your experience of life. Of the thousands of thoughts we have each day, how many of them do we consciously choose for ourselves?

In this exercise, you are invited to create a Mind Script for each of the three addictions that you are working on. A Mind Script is a written description of the thoughts you want to feed your mind every day. By reading your Mind Script daily, you are beginning to immerse your mind in the new beliefs that make up your ULS. This process is different from a pep talk or self-affirmation because the intent is not to change who you are. Rather, it is to accept who you are as you are.

Here are some helpful tips for Mind Scripting:

Write & speak with emotion

Your dominant thoughts are the ones that your mind will respond to most. The mind will automatically begin to translate into reality any thought you repeat with emotion. Most research on the power of the mind has acknowledged the importance of this principle. Emotions energize your thoughts. If you want your Mind Script to have a significant effect, it is important that you inject your thoughts with emotion while writing and saying them.

Use the present tense

When you write your Mind Scripts, declare your freedom now. Describe your ULS as if you are already experiencing it in this moment. The subconscious mind constantly prioritizes what it believes is most important to you right now. To have immediate effect, write or speak in the present tense using terms such as "I am," "I have," "I feel," or "I know" and avoid statements like "I will," "I want," "I desire," or "I can."

Speak out

While Mind Scripting, be sure to say the words out loud. This helps impress thoughts on the mind. As well, it is important to speak with conviction. Don't worry if you experience some doubts in the beginning. Your faith will naturally build over time as you do more and more of the exercises.

Keep it spontaneous

When you read your Mind Script it is important that it does not become monotonous. To prevent this exercise and any of the others from becoming meaningless rituals, view each of them as a catalyst for fresh revelations. Try to let your Mind Scripting evoke new ideas and new feelings. The eventual hope is that you will rid yourself of your dependence on a written Mind Script altogether and engage in Mind Scripting whenever and wherever you choose. The truth is that you can feed your mind liberating thoughts at any moment whether you are driving a car, putting out the garbage, or shopping for groceries.

Mind Scripting is the indispensable process of regularly immersing your mind in the new thoughts you wish to realize. You are what you think you are. If you think in terms of the ULS, you will experience just that. Remember, this is your life. Why not experience it your way! That is what Mind Scripting is all about – taking control and reinventing the possibilities.

For examples of this exercise, please refer to the next page.

MIND SCRIPTING – EXAMPLES

Acceptance of Others Addiction:

I am worthy of love as I am. I no longer need other people to accept me because I accept myself. I no longer need the respect of others for I have the respect of myself. I am now free to be myself in all my interactions with people. Rather than exhausting my energy worrying about what others think, I am now free to listen to my conscience and trust myself.

Comparison Addiction:

I am worthy of love regardless of whether I am the best or how I compare with others. I am now free to channel the time and energy I spent comparing myself to others into discovering who I am and unleashing my spirit. The people with whom I once compared myself with are now my allies. Instead of competing with others, I look for ways that we can draw upon each other's strengths. In this way their strengths become my strengths and together we grow more than we could alone.

Perfection Addiction:

I am worthy of love even if I am not perfect. Perfection is a myth – a recipe for misery. There are no more ideals. Even this exercise becomes worthless the minute it becomes a measure of my self-worth. There is no perfect way to think, look, act, and no perfect way to spend my time. I am now free to view my mistakes as opportunities to learn and grow. I can now accept myself for who I am, and realize the freedom to be me.

LUCID LIVING

Nothing happens unless first we dream.
> CARL SANDBURG

Have you ever moved into a new home? If so, what were some of the things you considered while furnishing your new place? Most likely, you carefully selected each piece of new furniture taking into account how its size, color, function and style might affect the overall ambiance you were trying to create. You invested time in this because your home is important to you. The way it is furnished affects the way you feel. Yet, how much time do you spend carefully choosing the images that decorate the chambers of your mind? Most of us spend no time at all. Instead, we let the forces of society define the visual elements that shape our feelings. Consequently, many of the images stored in our heads serve to reinforce our CLS Addictions. If you challenge these images with visions that reflect new possibilities for your life, you will help yourself break out of the web of your addictions.

A lucid dream occurs when you become conscious of the fact that you are dreaming and choose to participate in your dream while asleep. Just as you can influence the events of your dream world through the power of your thoughts, you can also influence your experience of life by consciously feeding your mind visualizations related to the ULS. Whenever you do this, you are Lucid Living.

Lucid Living empowers you to use the principle of visual imaging to break free from the limitations of your CLS Addictions.

Visualization tools are used by many top athletes to prepare for peak performance during games. The mind thinks in images, and those images define for us what is and is not possible. In Lucid Living you will feed your mind visual images charged with positive emotion to help reclaim your personal freedom.

Complete the following steps for each of the addictions you are working on:

1) Imagine the desired outcome

Close your eyes and suppose that you were free from this addiction. How would you feel? What would be the outcome? What would you be able to do and experience as a consequence of your freedom?

2) Draw what you see

While visualizing the possibilities, draw whatever images come to your mind. Don't worry, you do not need to be Michelangelo to do this. It does not matter how accurate your depictions are. What matters most is that they remind you of the vision you have in mind.

3) Describe the benefits

Identify the advantages of realizing the freedom that you have visualized for yourself. Try to be as specific and vivid as possible.

4) Start visualizing

Once you have created your Lucid Living visualizations, start using them daily by closing your eyes and visualizing yourself experiencing each benefit described. Use the pictures you have drawn and the feelings you have described to help you. The more vivid your visualizations are, the more effectively you will reinforce the ULS. It is also essential to believe in what you visualize. The stronger your convictions are, the greater the likelihood of eventually translating your vision into reality.

In order to maximize the impact of Lucid Living, repetition is necessary. The more you revisit each visualization, the more you will enhance its effects on your mind and your actual life experiences. Do not make the mistake of underestimating this tool. Repetition of your Lucid Living tool will positively transform your response to similar circumstances in the future.

What you can realize and experience in the ULS will depend on your willingness to imagine creative new possibilities for your life. Will you cling to the shore of the familiar and known CLS, or will you surrender to the tides of a new love that knows no bounds? The choice is yours.

For examples of this exercise, please refer to the next page.

MIND TRANSFORMATION

LUCID LIVING – EXAMPLES

DESIRED OUTCOME: Freedom from the Acceptance of Others addiction

VISUALIZATION #1

BENEFITS:

I feel relaxed to be myself even around those who are quick to judge me.

For The Reader's Benefit
Explanation of Visualization #1:
In the example above, the man visualizes the judgments of other people as smoke in their minds. He sees that the smoke has nothing to do with him. It comes from their ideas of who he is. He imagines the force of his unconditional self-love shielding him from the smoke so that he does not waste any more energy worrying about what other people think.

VISUALIZATION #2

BENEFITS:

I feel free from the fear and anxiety that came from needing to say what others wanted to hear. I am in a state of complete acceptance and peace.

For The Reader's Benefit
Explanation of Visualization #2:
In the example above, the man visualizes himself standing in front of an audience sharing his views. He sees that some people are approving and some are not. In either case, he is not affected because he accepts himself as he is and no longer needs the acceptance of others.

181

D-Mapping

The thoughts, images, and emotions that dominate your mind will shape the quality of your life experience. It is as simple as that. In fact, this pretty much summarizes the three principles of the mind discussed earlier.

(1) You are what you think you are.
(2) You are what you imagine yourself to be.
(3) Your mind responds best to emotion.

A D-Map is a visual representation of what the ULS means to you. It incorporates each of these principles to evoke a powerful mental and emotional transformation within your life.

To begin this process, simply imagine what you would think and feel if you truly realized, with all your heart, that you are worthy of love and acceptance as you are. After jotting down some initial ideas, find a large poster-size sheet of paper. If necessary, tape two smaller pieces of paper together.

1) At the heart of this map depict your Central Unconditional Love Belief (CULB) of "I am worthy of love and acceptance as I am." Be as creative as you want and depict the concept any way you please. You may choose to draw a circle in the center of your page where you write the words in bold letters. You may also choose to include a picture that best represents this belief. Whatever image you choose, ensure that it is symbolic and meaningful to you.

2) Surround the CULB with the Unconditional Love Responses (ULRs) you have uncovered in the Exploring the ULS exercise. Be sure to leave some room for the other addictions you will explore in the future. Write down these beliefs in bold lettering and, where possible, find images that you feel best illustrate each respective belief. If you cannot find images that suit your preference, you may want to draw them yourself. Don't worry about your artistic skills. It does not have to be an accurate depiction. What matters most is that the images inspire corresponding emotions in your mind.

3) Meditate on the qualities, feelings, or thoughts that each of the ULRs inspire. For example, the ULR of "I am worthy of love regardless of how others perceive me," might inspire the quality of courage in your mind. If so, you would depict courage on your D-Map with words or images. If you want you can also include quotations that inspire you. You may also choose to select images of people that symbolize this attribute.

It is very easy to lose track of what is important to us in our lives. Distractions surround us. We are bombarded by images and words wherever we go. By taking a few moments each day to meditate on your D-Map, you will be reminded of what is most important to you. Since the images and words have significance to you, observing them will have an immediate effect on your mind. The emotional charge behind each image and word will contribute to reclaiming your personal freedom and reinforcing the ULS in your heart and mind.

While developing your D-Map feel free to think outside the box and channel your creativity in any way you desire. The "D" in D-Mapping stands for Destiny. By creating and using your D-Map you are taking valuable steps towards realizing a destiny that you have chosen for yourself. This destiny that we refer to has nothing to do with striving for a better future. It is about making each moment your destiny through realizing a complete freedom to be yourself.

For examples of this exercise, please refer to the next page.

Since D-Mapping is a visual representation of what the ULS means to you, it is a process that never ends. As you explore the freedom of unconditional self-love, you will keep discovering new things about yourself. This continual evolution will broaden your vision and enrich the D-Map of your life. Using your D-Map as a source of creative meditation is a powerful reinforcement of the thoughts, images, and emotions that the ULS inspires in you.

A Helpful Tip

If finding pictures is difficult for you, take advantage of technology. With the help of the internet and color printers, finding appropriate images is inexpensive and easy. Simply go to a popular search engine and run an image search on whomever or whatever you would like to find. You will instantly find images that you may print for your non-commercial purposes.

D-Mapping – Example*

COURAGE

(I am worthy of love regardless of what other people think of me.)

FOLLOW MY HEART

GROWTH

(I am worthy of love regardless of whether I am successful.)

(I am worthy of love regardless of the mistakes I may make.)

(**I AM WORTHY OF LOVE AS I AM**)

(I am worthy of love regardless of whether I am productive.)

(I am worthy of love regardless of how I compare with others.)

(I am worthy of love regardless of whether I find someone to spend my life with.)

ENJOYING THE JOURNEY

FREE TO BE MYSELF

SELF-LOVE

* Images can be used in place of or in addition to the words. This is your D-Map, so feel free to visually represent the ULS in any way you please.

Part 3

MANIFESTATION

Liberation Through Action

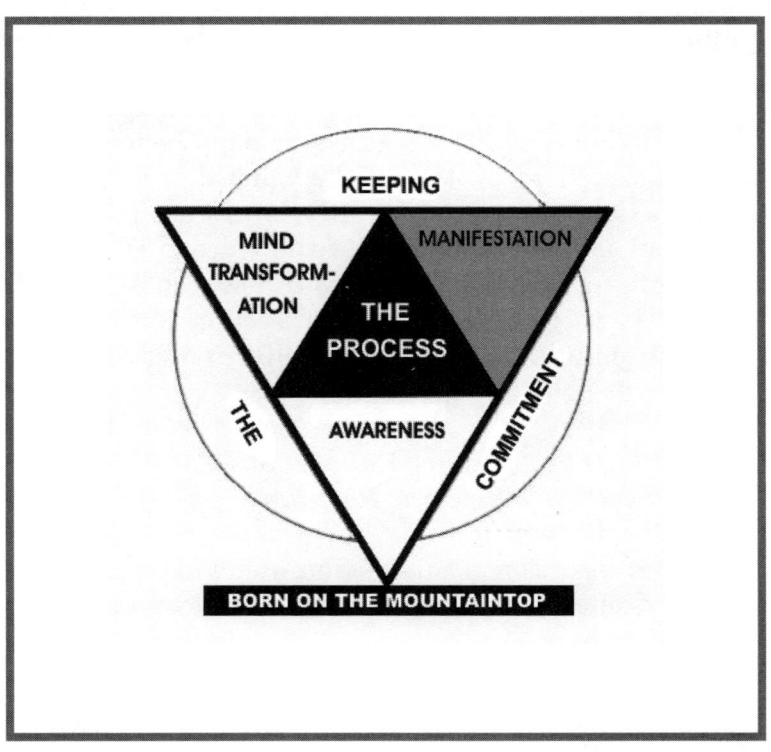

MANIFESTATION

In the Awareness section, you explored your CLS Addictions and the revolutionary impact of the ULS. The Mind Transformation section has provided the insights and techniques required to trigger a transformation in the way you think and feel. These are huge steps that help you to feel worthy of love no matter what. As you begin to change your perception of yourself, you will naturally be inclined to express this newfound freedom in action. The Manifestation section is about learning how to express the freedom of the ULS in what you say and do.

How you interact within the world sends powerful signals to your mind and heart that help affirm or deny beliefs about who you are. If your actions contradict the belief that you are worthy of love as you are, you will never fully experience the freedom of the ULS. That is why this phase of the journey is dedicated to helping you align your actions with your newly chosen beliefs.

In the first part of the Manifestation section, you will practice expressing unconditional love to yourself through the use of the following tools:

Breaking Free by Choosing Your Actions
Unconditional Love Rewards Program

In the remaining portion of this section, you will uncover the following ways of expressing unconditional love to others:

Creating Safe Spaces
Perceptual Shifts
Saying the Words
Sharing Your Experiences

Rewarding Others with Unconditional Love
Releasing the Past with Others

When you let the **ULS** guide your actions in the world, you will enrich the quality of your relationships with yourself and others.

LOVE OF SELF

BREAKING FREE BY CHOOSING YOUR ACTIONS

What we call the secret to happiness is no more a secret than our willingness to choose life.

LEO BUSCAGLIA

In the past satisfying your CLS Addictions was likely your predominant way of experiencing love and acceptance. After years of engaging in addictive behavior, it can be challenging to break free from these habits and embrace a new way. But, consider the consequences of not breaking free. You will spend the remainder of your life trying to prove that you are worthy of your own self-respect. Breaking Free by Choosing Your Actions is a tool designed to help you overcome the habit of fulfilling CLS Addictions.

To understand this exercise, suppose that you have an Acceptance of Others addiction and have been applying all the Mind Transformation tools towards breaking free from it. By using these tools you notice significant changes in the way you perceive life. At times, however, you still find yourself seeking the acceptance of others through your actions. What are the consequences of this? Every time you perform Conditional Love Actions (CLAs), you are reinforcing your addictions. As a result, you find yourself sending contradictory messages to yourself. On one level, you are reinforcing the ULS through the Mind Transformation tools. Yet, on another level, you are reinforcing the CLS through your actions.

How can you address this dilemma? When you feel yourself being pulled by old CLS habits and behaving according to your addictions, it is essential to have a technique that can help you. The following technique will enable you to avert the habitual nature of your addictions:

1) Change your Emotional State

Fear is the predominant emotion of the CLS. If you want to break free from Conditional Love Actions (CLAs), you must first break free from the fear that compels you to do them. To do this you can apply the principle of association to your advantage. Have you ever heard a song that immediately reminded you of your past? Did the song also bring back past emotions? When this happens, the song is associated so strongly with these emotions that it triggers the same feelings in the present.

Whether you are aware of it or not, the last four Mind Transformation tools help create powerful associations in your mind. The emotions of unconditional love that you experience while applying each tool become associated with the visualizations or words you are using. All the words and images of these tools are charged with the positive emotions you have associated with them over time. By recalling them, you activate those same emotions inside you that have the power to push your fears aside. For example, you could resolve the fear you feel in a situation by recalling parts of your Mind Script. Or you could also use a Lucid Living visualization to evoke the feelings of unconditional love you have developed for yourself.

2) Affirm the Choice

Now that you have altered your emotional state, inwardly say the words "I choose to be worthy of love as I am." This particular phrase is especially effective because it will remind you that acting in accordance with your ULS is nothing more than a choice. This reminder is empowering as it acknowledges that this choice is completely in your hands at every moment.

3) Just Do It

Use the momentum from steps 1 and 2 above to act out your ULA. Even if you feel hesitant, just give yourself a push to do it. Do not underestimate the significance of your every action. Each time you apply this tool, you are taking an essential step towards breaking free from the habitual hold of your addictions. Regardless of the outcome, every ULA strengthens your ability to live and love without conditions. In this respect, your freedom is just a choice away.

Unconditional Love Rewards Program

You yourself, as much as anybody in the entire universe, deserve your love and affection.

The Buddha

When you love someone you likely express this love in many ways. However, how often do you get a chance to express love to yourself? Most of us reward ourselves only when we have a good reason or feel deserving of it. Often we wait for some special occasion like a birthday or an achievement. Though this may seem natural, there is a serious problem with this. Rewarding ourselves is a way of expressing acceptance and love to ourselves. If we only reward ourselves when we prove ourselves worthy, we are reinforcing the CLS. We must find a better way to communicate our appreciation to ourselves that reflects the unconditional love of the ULS.

The Unconditional Love Rewards Program is a revolutionary approach to expressing love and acceptance to yourself. It requires that you reward yourself regularly for absolutely no reason at all! Even when things do not work out the way you wanted or when you fail in every respect, you are still going to reward yourself. At first, this may seem absurd, perhaps even crazy. In fact, you might wonder how it is even possible to be kind to yourself under such circumstances. But, you only feel this way because you have been conditioned to believe that you do not deserve love until you prove yourself worthy of it.

The Unconditional Love Rewards Program is one of the most effective ways of communicating the message of unconditional love to yourself. When you reward yourself, you prove that you are indeed capable of expressing love to yourself without a reason, and that the freedom of the ULS is yours to choose. Every time you do this, you make a profound impression on yourself that dismisses any doubt regarding the possibility of the ULS.

Take the time now to develop your own Unconditional Love Rewards Program by making a list of ways in which you can express love to yourself. At first, you may find this task difficult especially if you have never rewarded yourself without a reason.

Do it anyways. There is far too much to gain from this simple act. Once you get going, you will not only get the hang of it, but look forward to it.

These rewards do not necessarily require spending money. One of the students of the Born on the Mountaintop course realized that he expressed love to others by believing in them and listening to them carefully. But, he did not do the same for himself. He decided to make listening to himself and believing in himself his Unconditional Love Rewards.

If you want, you can also divide your list into daily, weekly, and monthly rewards. The choice is yours. There are no set rules, except that you must give yourself these rewards regularly for absolutely no reason at all. Enjoy.

A Helpful Tip

Another very effective way of using the Unconditional Love Rewards Program is to take a moment of silence every day to ask yourself: "What can I do to express love to myself today?" Try to act on whatever answer comes to you. Do not underestimate this technique. It is amazing how even the most seemingly insignificant action can help you experience the profound feeling of being worthy of love as you are.

LOVE OF OTHERS

Freedom and love go together. Love is not a reaction. If I love you because you love me, that is mere trade, a thing to be bought in the market; it is not love. To love is not to ask anything in return, not even to feel that you are giving something – and it is only such love that can know freedom.

JIDDU KRISHNAMURTI

Everywhere we go, the belief that we need to prove our worth is being reinforced. Just as you have developed addictions because of this belief, so have others. Most people are not aware that they have addictions, yet much of what they are doing is coming from a search for love and acceptance. In our interactions with others, how can we give others a much-needed break from this never-ending struggle to prove their worth? Now that you have begun to experience the ULS, how can you communicate to people that they are also worthy of love as they are? Up until this point, all the exercises and tools have focused on developing unconditional love for yourself. This section will now discuss how you can express unconditional love to others.

How you treat others affects the way you treat yourself, and how you treat yourself affects the way you treat others. Both are deeply interconnected. Every time you communicate to others that they are not worthy of love and acceptance as they are, you reinforce this Central Conditional Love Belief (CCLB) in yourself. In some cases, the conditions you place on the love and acceptance of yourself are often the same conditions you place on others.

Naturally, it will take some effort and practice to express unconditional love for others, especially when most of us struggle to express such love to ourselves. For this reason, we advise you to do the following exercises only when you feel ready for them.

CREATING SAFE SPACES

If you judge people, you have no time to love them.
                              MOTHER TERESA

Have you ever noticed that the people we are most comfortable with are the ones that let us be who we are? To find people who accept us for who we are is rare because we live in a world where we judge each other constantly. The reason for this is simple. Just as we place conditions on our own acceptance in the CLS, we also tend to place conditions on the love we give to others. Whenever people do not meet our criteria of acceptability we judge them. Not surprisingly, people feel restricted in what they say and do.

By affirming the belief that we are all worthy of love as we are, you will be in a unique position to create safe spaces for the people with whom you interact. Safe spaces are environments where people feel free to be themselves without the fear of being judged. To create this environment for others all you have to do is start letting go of your criteria for accepting others.

By accepting people you give them the rare opportunity to have someone listen to them without judgment. This gives people the confidence to let their guard down to express their innermost feelings. You may be surprised to learn that certain people have felt inhibited to share parts of themselves with you. They may have felt you would not have accepted them based on your conditions for loving them. When people feel free to share themselves, you are able to understand them on a totally different level. When you create safe spaces this enriches the relationship and allows you to appreciate others for who they really are.

Often people in a romantic relationship will ask each other "Why do you love me?" They cannot believe that anyone could love them without a reason. They want to know how they have come to prove themselves worthy of the love they enjoy. Unconditional love does not require anyone to prove anything. The love is given freely because it is given by those who are free to love without expectations. Creating safe spaces helps us finally support and love the people in our lives. It eliminates the unfair demands we place on people and allows us to finally build the relationships we want.

Perceptual Shifts

How you perceive others can affect the way they perceive you. People are sensitive to the judgments of others. In fact, without you saying a single word, others can detect how you feel about them. These thoughts and emotions are conveyed through our body language and are detected consciously or subconsciously by the people with whom we interact. One of the simplest ways we can express unconditional love to others is by taking advantage of this principle. Whether meeting friends or strangers, you can help them feel unconditional love by inwardly repeating the words, "You are worthy of love as you are," when you meet them. This shift in your perception of them will be conveyed in the way you treat them. They may not know what exactly has changed, but they will feel and appreciate the difference because you are accepting them in a way that few people do – without conditions.

Saying the Words

Embrace every opportunity to express your unconditional love. With full conviction, do not hesitate to say the words, "You are worthy of love as you are," or "I love you as you are." Too often, we wait until it is too late to express our love to others. We find ourselves uncovering the depths of our true feelings for others when they are sick or have left our lives. Life is too short to remain distant from the people we love. Expressing unconditional love in words can have an immediate effect on how others feel and open them to a new way of experiencing love.

> ## *Satyam's Corner*
> ## The Universal Language of Love
>
> I can remember talking on the phone with a close friend who was very distressed by the possibility of failing at something important to her. She had reached a point where the stress was making her hyperventilate. I had tried to calm her down with breathing techniques, but it did not change anything. Finally, I closed my eyes and spoke from my heart. I told her that even if she failed or made a complete fool of herself, I still loved her. The effect was immediate. Her breathing changed and she calmed down. It was a moment of complete honesty and true friendship. The experience helped me understand the healing power of expressing unconditional love. The language of the ULS is universal. People may not know about the CLS or the ULS, but when they feel unconditional love they immediately appreciate it. When you make a Perceptual Shift or Say the Words to someone, it can transform them because you are finally giving them the love they long for.

SHARING YOUR EXPERIENCES

And as we let our own light shine, we unconsciously give other people permission to do the same. As we are liberated from our fear, our presence automatically liberates others.

MARIANNE WILLIAMSON

Once you appreciate your own addictions and where they are coming from, you will notice that everyone has much more in common than you realized. Much of the stress and fear we all experience is coming from the common central belief of the CLS. We are all searching for the same love and acceptance. By finding the courage to share your personal experiences with others, you might inspire and encourage people to break free from their addictions. Sharing is a wonderful experience, but many of us refrain from disclosing our deepest thoughts and emotions because we are afraid that others might pass judgment on us. However, there is a law of reciprocity that prevails in human communication. This law dictates that the people you associate with will be as open with you as you are with them. You will be amazed to discover that when you break free from the fear of how others may react and bear your vulnerabilities to another, you will give others the courage to do the same. By sharing your personal experiences you will open people's minds and hearts to their own conditioning and the opportunities made possible through the ULS.

> ### The Invisible Elephant
>
> During a follow-up session, a student of the Born on the Mountaintop course explained that when she learned about the CLS and ULS it was like an invisible elephant had been exposed. She felt as if she had spent her entire life with this invisible elephant in the room. Everyone felt its presence, but no one said anything about it. For her, Born on the Mountaintop revealed the elephant, and she wondered why people did not talk about these issues before. All this time, she felt alone in her struggle to gain love and acceptance, but after hearing other people's experiences she came to understand that we all feel the CLS in our lives, just in different ways. Sharing Your Experiences means talking about that invisible elephant whose presence we all sense, but do not get a chance to acknowledge or explore.

Rewarding Others With Unconditional Love

In the Unconditional Love Rewards Program, you came up with ways to express love for yourself. Now you are invited to explore ways of expressing such unconditional love to others. The more frequently people experience love without conditions, the more they will believe themselves worthy of love as they are. That is why loving others unconditionally can have such a positive impact on people's lives.

There are countless ways of expressing your unconditional love. You are limited only by your imagination. Some examples include:

Listening without judgment

Everyone's thoughts and feelings are important. If you can take the time to make people feel their importance you have made a positive difference. Also, listening without judgment is a supreme act of love.

Therapeutic Touch

People hunger for affection, yet are often afraid to ask for it. Human touch is an effective way of reaching out to people. If you are comfortable with touch, hold the hands of close friends and relatives. Hugging is also an effective way of expressing affection. Massaging is also therapeutic as it helps release tension from the body.

Making something

You do not need to buy a gift to express your love to someone. People tend to appreciate receiving something handmade more. Have you ever noticed how much it means to some people when a child simply draws a picture and dedicates it to them? We're not suggesting that you pull out your crayons, but you can let your creativity go and show someone that they matter by making something for them. Making something for someone shows that you care enough to dedicate your time and energy into physically expressing your love.

Writing your thoughts and feelings

In this age of emails, it is rare to receive a handwritten letter. However, most people appreciate a handwritten letter more than an email because they value the time and effort taken to write it.

There are really no limits to what you can do. All that matters is that rewards are given without a reason and without expecting anything in return.

Another important consideration while Rewarding Others With Unconditional Love is to be sensitive to the ways in which different people like to be loved. Everyone is unique with their own set of preferences. That is why taking the time to discover what a person appreciates will make your love better received. This is where your creativity and investigation skills will come in handy. Have fun with this tool. You are venturing into a new frontier of interaction that will enrich your relationships.

RELEASING THE PAST WITH OTHERS

In the Mind Transformation phase of the journey, you released the hurt of your addictive past. Now you will be asked to acknowledge the transgressions you have made towards others. You may recall that we defined a transgression as any thought or action that reinforces the message of "I am not worthy of love as I am."

In this exercise you will reflect on your past and recall instances when you communicated this message to others. Reflect on the significant relationships you have had in your life. Consider how your actions towards these people may have enforced the idea that they need to be something other than themselves to be worthy of your love. The intention of this exercise is not to feel guilty about what you did, but to acknowledge how you have hurt others.

For examples of this exercise, please refer to the end of this section.

Acknowledging how your actions are received will deepen your sensitivity towards others in the future. This process will also help you come to realize that your addictions have not only harmed you, but they have harmed most relationships you have had.

Once you have completed your list of transgressions, the next step involves apologizing to the people on your list. If you are not ready for this step it can be saved for a later time. Be sure to only apologize when you feel comfortable and capable of doing so as described below.

Making Appointments

After you have completed your list, make appointments with the people listed in order to apologize face-to-face for the transgressions you committed. Of all the exercises, this is among the most difficult and rewarding. It is no minor feat to disclose your shortcomings to another. It takes great courage.

While you apologize, insist that you are not interrupted. Be sure to specify exactly how you have reinforced the hurtful message of conditional love through your actions. The people you apologize to will benefit from the process because it gives them an opportunity to release any negative feelings they may have associated with the incident. The apology might also help them clarify the past and alleviate any blame they may have wrongfully credited to themselves.

Under most circumstances, you will find that apologizing to others is rewarding and that most people you apologize to will appreciate your efforts. Nonetheless, the following advice has been provided to help you avoid any potential disputes.

Be careful to avoid engaging in any form of confrontation while delivering your apology. No one can deny that others have hurt you, just as you have hurt others. You may even find that some of the people you apologize to actually have more reason to apologize to you. However, keep in mind that your purpose is to apologize for your actions. You are not apologizing to point out the shortcomings of another. Since you do not want to repeat the past, it is important for you to remain calm and vigilant even when met with extreme resistance in the form of anger, accusation, misunderstanding and pride. While apologizing, refrain from using the word "you" as it can seem accusatory.

It may happen that, despite your best intentions, a person you apologize to refuses to accept your apology. Do not take this rejection personally. At all costs, avoid arguing about the past. You are not there to win an argument. You are on a specific mission to acknowledge your transgressions so that you and others may reap the benefits of apologizing.

Start with someone who you feel close to. If by chance you are incapable of talking to someone, you can use your faculties of visualization. Close your eyes and imagine the person before you. Then apologize in the above manner to their image. This psychological technique can allow you to reap many of the benefits of an actual face-to-face encounter, provided you conduct the apology with the utmost sincerity.

When you apologize while Releasing the Past with Others, you not only help others heal themselves, you also contribute to your own healing. Most of the transgressions you have committed to others have been caused by your CLS Addictions. These addictions have hurt you as much as they have hurt other people in your life. Acknowledging them in any way releases any guilt or hurt and affirms your resolve to change in the future.

RELEASING THE PAST WITH OTHERS – EXAMPLE

CLS VICTIM	CIRCUMSTANCE	TRANSGRESSIONS TO OTHERS
SPOUSE	When we had arguments over our wedding anniversary arrangements.	I withdrew my affection for him during our disagreements. I hurt him by making him feel that he had to agree with my way of doing things to be worthy of my love.
FATHER	When he disapproved of my career decision.	I withdrew my love and affection for him at the time because I was really upset. Looking back, I recognize that he had every right to express his opinion. I was the one who was incapable of respecting his opinion while respecting my own. I sent him the message that he was not acceptable unless he met my expectations of him.
BROTHER	When we were younger and he did not meet my expectations of him.	I made him feel less worthy of love when he did not meet my high expectations of him. During such circumstances, I stopped talking to him and refused to share anything with him.
SISTER	When I disapproved of her boyfriend.	I was completely unsupportive of her relationship with this man. I made her feel like she was doing something wrong simply because I did not approve of her decision. I indirectly sent her the message that unless she dated someone I approved of, she was not worthy of my love.
COLLEAGUE	When I took her contributions for granted during a major project at work.	I did not show any appreciation for my colleague's significant contributions to the project. I was so consumed in getting the job done that I only focused on her shortcomings. I kept getting upset whenever she made a mistake. Sometimes I may have been too harsh. My behavior has made her feel that she will only be accepted when she is perfect.

SOME COMMONLY ASKED QUESTIONS

How do I change other people so they, too, can live in the ULS?

As you start to feel love and acceptance for yourself, it is natural to want others to change so that they can also experience the ULS. This is, however, a misguided ambition. When you try to change others, you tell them they are not worthy of love as they are. If they were worthy, you would not require them to change anything about themselves. Every time you try to change others, you hurt them at the deepest level because you are enforcing the beliefs that create so much anguish and discontent in their lives.

If I can't change them, is there any way I can help them?

If someone you knew was engaging in self-destructive behavior, wouldn't you do something about it? For example, if your divorced friend was depressed and unable to accept herself due to her marriage falling apart, would you stand by and do nothing? Unconditional love may inspire you to accept and support your friend throughout her depression. Your love may also encourage you to challenge her CLS in a non-confrontational way. Unconditional love does not necessarily mean being passive. Instead, it can be an active force that reaches out to others in a spirit of compassion. The motive of this love is not to change others, but to show them an alternative to the CLS and assure them they are worthy of love as they are. You are also encouraged to use the tools that you learned in the Love of Others section. They are effective, non-confrontational ways of letting people experience unconditional love.

How do I deal with people who are making me or others feel less worthy of love?

Given that we live in a world dominated by a CLS consciousness, many of the people you encounter will have difficulty accepting you as you are. Among such people, there will be those who will go out of their way to put you down or provoke you. When you encounter people behaving in this way, you have a choice to either silently accept their transgression to you, or you can break the silence with your insight into the ULS. Most people choose to stay quiet to avoid confrontations that might lead to others negatively judging them. This choice is made from a fear of what others may think. Breaking the silence takes courage. If done in a spirit of unconditional love, breaking the silence has nothing to do with imposing your views on others. When done with love, there is no desire to change the other person or need for them to accept your views. Even if they misunderstand or reject your efforts, your unconditional love gives you the strength and freedom to continue loving them and yourself.

Often you will find yourself in situations where you experience hurt due to someone else's behavior. When you experience such pain, the most common reaction is to become defensive and reactive. For example, if someone criticizes you, you may be tempted to lash out by criticizing him. You may want to blame the other person for hurting you. However, when you analyze your addictions, you will find that your hurt is not coming from other people. For example, if people criticize you, you are often hurt by their behavior because of a need to be accepted by them. When you are free from this need to be accepted, you can withstand the abuse of others while continuing to love yourself.

Compassion for the other person will also help you see the situation differently. When you understand that people's abusive behavior is usually a consequence of their own addictions, it is easier to forgive their transgressions against you and others. The deep need for love can manifest in desperate ways for certain individuals. In fact, usually the more destructive a person is the more he or she is starving for love.

If there is a solution to these problems, it cannot be found in lashing out or judging the person who is abusive. These reactions only reinforce the idea that others need to prove themselves worthy of our love. That is why the best way to help people is by giving them unconditional love. Although this is difficult and takes courage, acting otherwise will only strengthen their addictions and make the problem worse.

Please note that this discussion is not about creating new ideals for how you should behave. The primary intent of this investigation is to help deepen your awareness of your own behavior and the choices available to you.

Making It Happen

Knowing is not enough, we must apply.
Willing is not enough, we must do.
Bruce Lee

Congratulations on completing the first three parts of the journey. You have now learned the tools that will help you reclaim the freedom of the ULS in your thoughts, feelings, and actions. If you are like most of the people who make it this far, you are probably anxious to apply everything you have learned. Though we commend your enthusiasm, we do not recommend that you try to apply all the tools at once. This would be both overwhelming and ineffective. That is why we have divided the implementation of the tools into the following two phases.

Phase One

The primary objective of the first phase is to focus on exploring and experiencing how it feels to be worthy of love and acceptance as you are. To assist this process, we recommend you use the following tools for the three addictions you have selected.

> *The Awareness Journal*
> *Releasing the Past*
> *Tapping into the ULS*
> *The Unconditional Love Rewards Program*

In this phase, all that you are being asked to do is open your mind and heart to the possibility of loving and accepting yourself as you are. In the Awareness Journal you have the opportunity to understand how the CLS is affecting you and explore new possibilities for your life in the ULS. By Releasing the Past, you will become more aware of the dominant role the CLS plays in your life and heal yourself from the hurt it has caused. In Tapping into the ULS you will practice opening yourself up to the feeling of unconditional self-love. Lastly, by rewarding yourself through the Unconditional Love Rewards Program you will experience the transformative power of expressing love to yourself for absolutely no reason.

Notice that none of these suggested tools focus on breaking free from individual addictions. The central belief of the ULS says that you are worthy of love as you are. This involves a revolutionary change in your perspective, and it is important to give yourself time to grasp its complete significance. This phase encourages you to engage in experimentation, reflection and soul-searching. If you skip this process and make your primary focus breaking free from your addictions, you will run the risk of basing your worth on how free you are. This would contradict the essence of the ULS entirely. It is important to understand that you are worthy of love even if you are not free from your addictions. Letting yourself experience the profound self-love of the ULS, no matter what, is the focus of this first stage.

Of course, you can use the other tools whenever you like, as long as your primary focus in this first phase is exploring and building a new center of unconditional love within yourself. We recommend that you officially move on to the next phase only after you are able to avoid the tendency of basing your self-worth on breaking free from your addictions.

Phase Two

The purpose of this phase is to help you break free from your CLS Addictions in a spirit of compassion and self-love. In addition to using the tools of Phase One, you have the flexibility of using any of the following tools to strengthen your realization of the ULS. Again, start by applying them only on the three addictions you have selected.

Mind Transformation tools:
Mind Scripting
Lucid Living
D-Mapping

Manifestation tools:
Breaking Free by Choosing Your Actions
Creating Safe Spaces
Perceptual Shifts

Saying the Words
Sharing Your Experiences
Rewarding Others With Unconditional Love
Releasing the Past With Others

The Mind Transformation tools allow you to use the principles of the mind to break free from your addictions. Once you build your Mind Scripts, Lucid Living visualizations and D-Map, regularly use the tools to transform your thoughts and emotions. The Manifestation tools allow you to experience the freedom of the ULS in action. You can use Breaking Free by Choosing Your Actions to start implementing the choices you discover in the ULS. The remaining tools help open the door to richer relationships with others.

Realistically, you will only need to spend about 30-45 minutes a day on the program. In the morning we recommend you allot 15-30 minutes to Tapping into your ULS, saying your Mind Scripts, doing your Lucid Living visualizations and meditating on your D-Map. At the end of each day, we suggest you dedicate approximately 15 minutes towards your Awareness Journal. Throughout the day, you are encouraged to express unconditional love to others and yourself through your actions.

As you realize the freedom possible through these tools, we recommend you apply them to other addictions you may have. If you want to make a stronger commitment, by all means feel free to spend more time on the exercises or do them more frequently. Ultimately, the benefits you reap will be in proportion to what you are prepared to put in.

Part 4

Keeping the Commitment

Staying the Course

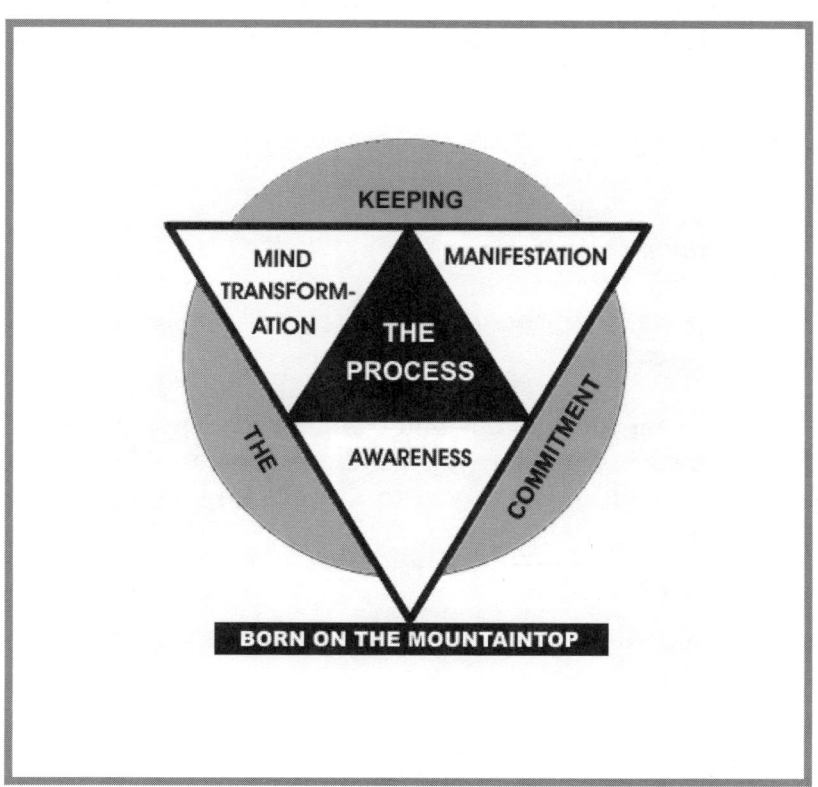

Keeping The Commitment

Keeping a commitment to ourselves is not always an easy task. Despite our best of intentions, most of us struggle to honor the commitments we make to ourselves. However, if you wish to continue experiencing the benefits of the Mind Transformation and Manifestation tools you need to develop a sound strategy for overcoming whatever stands in the way between you and the life you want. Keeping the Commitment is the final part of our journey together. The purpose of this section is to show you how you can honor your commitments to the ULS. By reading on, you will learn how to find the time, energy, motivation, and discipline to reclaim your personal freedom every day. Within this section you will explore the following tools and insights to sustain your commitments:

>*Keeping Yourself Motivated*
>*Removing Obstacles*
>*Lifestyle Integration*
>*Tracking Your Commitments*
>*Self-Coaching*

If you are someone who has had trouble with staying motivated and disciplined in the past, you will be thrilled to know that the tools to come will empower you to achieve any goal you set for yourself.

KEEPING YOURSELF MOTIVATED

One of the biggest problems people face when trying to honor their commitments to themselves is staying motivated to continue over the long term. Motivation is your will to persevere, and it can vacillate depending on what you choose to think about. Most people would agree that choosing the right foods to eat is an essential part of health, but there is little discussion about what we feed our minds. Our mental diet has the greatest impact on our levels of motivation. Our minds are being constantly stimulated. Since society is entrenched in the CLS, the media and most of the people we meet reinforce ideas of needing to prove our worthiness of love and acceptance. As a result of these influences, our motivation for the ULS can be easily smothered. If you are not conscientious and selective about the influences you expose yourself to, you can end up reinforcing your addictions by sheer default. Obviously, there are influences you cannot avoid, but there are many that you can. That is why it is important for you to become aware of what you are currently feeding your mind. Evaluate whether the messages you are receiving are contributing to the positive changes you want to make. This analysis might inspire you to make some lifestyle changes. For example, you may decide to change some of the people you interact with, the television shows you watch or the things you read.

The ULS represents freedom in its absolute sense, but this freedom has a price. Realizing that you are worthy of love and acceptance as you are is a revolutionary way of living. It is not something that can be given to you. You must do the work. This means that you may have to go out of your way to seek new ideas that motivate you towards your freedom. You might do this by making a habit of reading, listening to audio-books and watching movies or documentaries that reinforce the freedom of the ULS. There are many fascinating people in this world who are leading inspiring lives. These people can be a great source of motivation and support as you learn to integrate the ULS into your life. Keep in mind that no one can know what is best for you but you. That is why we highly recommend you look at your mental diet and reassess what you feed your mind.

Removing Obstacles

No matter how motivated you are to realizing the ULS in your life, you will experience a great deal of frustration if you do not remove the obstacles that lie in your way. If the obstacles are unknown to you, your frustration may even lead you to abandon your commitment to the ULS. Knowing some of these obstacles in advance can minimize this frustration. Here are some of the major obstacles that you should be aware of:

1) Contradicting Desires

Sometimes we can make efforts to move towards one desire while simultaneously doing things that defeat these very efforts. One of the most common mistakes people make is having desires in the ULS while also upholding contradictory desires in the CLS. For example, one may desire to overcome his Acceptance of Others addiction while simultaneously making the effort to win the affection of his friends. These two contradicting goals reinforce contradicting beliefs in the mind and, consequently, create frustration. Although this may seem obvious, it actually takes a lot of awareness to catch yourself engaging in this type of contradictory behavior. Regular entries in your Awareness Journal will ensure you avoid this obstacle by keeping you in tune with the motivations behind your actions.

2) Lack of Self-Confidence

Positive action creates positive momentum. By applying the tools described throughout this book, you will experience the results for yourself and each positive experience will build your self-confidence. Since the ULS is new to your life, you are not expected to have immediate confidence in all that is possible. We encourage you, however, to jump into it. With every step you take, the results will increase your conviction in your power to choose the life you want. Soon you will get the hang of it and realize that complete self-love is indeed possible.

3) Self-Consciousness

Applying the insights and tools described in this book has a liberating effect and, in most cases, people will welcome the positive changes they see in you. Some may even want you to share what you have learned. At the same time, the ULS can require the courage to think and act outside what is commonly accepted by today's society. As you express your freedom, you will likely come across some people who are not familiar with your vision and who may not agree with what you are doing. Among those who disagree, some may even be critical of your views and feel threatened by the freedom you are giving yourself. In the face of this resistance, try not to let self-consciousness stand between you and the life you want.

LIFESTYLE INTEGRATION

When people feel they do not have time to do the things they want, it is often due to lack of motivation. In other cases, the solution lies in probing to find where that extra time and energy can be found. This is usually the case because most people have not been taught to strategically allocate their time and energy. Even people who are very productive still find that they spend a lot of time doing things that matter least to them.

The purpose of this section is to explore how you can find the time and energy to incorporate the Mind Transformation and Manifestation tools into your existing lifestyle. Before you can uncover realistic ways of making such integration possible, you need to become aware of how you actually spend your time and energy. To do this, observe yourself for one week and record how you spend each hour.

Once you have documented your activity for the week, it is time for you to uncover opportunities for integrating the tools of this program into your routine. Such opportunities will be easier to identify if you become familiar with the following concepts:

> **Time Vacuums:** Activities that seem intriguing, but actually end up sucking your time and preventing you from doing things that are more important to you.
>
> **Energy Vacuums:** Activities that drain your energy levels, leaving you physically, mentally, or emotionally exhausted.
>
> **Energy Amplifiers:** Activities that increase your energy levels by leaving you physically, mentally, or emotionally charged.
>
> **Multi-Tasking:** Managing the simultaneous execution of more than one task.
>
> **Substitution:** Replacing an activity with little or no meaning for something that is more important to you.

Acceleration: Engaging in more activities within the same allotment of time.

Study your weekly schedule to identify any activities that could be categorized as time vacuums, energy vacuums or energy amplifiers. Also look to identify any opportunities for multi-tasking, substitution and acceleration. Once you have identified such opportunities, look to integrate the tools of this program into your lifestyle wherever possible. If you want, engage in energy amplifiers wherever you notice your energy levels dropping throughout the day. For example, some people find regular exercise, yoga, meditation, sleep and inspirational music to be excellent ways of rejuvenating themselves. These amplifiers can help ensure you have enough energy to adequately meet the demands of your day.

This Lifestyle Integration tool challenges you to harness your self-awareness and creativity. By becoming aware of how you are currently allocating your time and energy, you will be in a position to creatively brainstorm ways of finding the time and energy needed to apply the ULS tools.

For an example of this exercise, please refer to the next page.

LIFESTYLE INTEGRATION – EXAMPLE

TIME OF DAY	MONDAY
7 – 8 AM	Get dressed & have breakfast
8 – 9 AM	Drive to work while listening to the radio
9 – 10 AM	Work
10 – 11 AM	Work
11 – 12 PM	Work
12 – 1 PM	Lunch in the cafeteria
1 – 2 PM	Work
2 – 3 PM	Work
3 – 4 PM	Work
4 – 5 PM	Work
5 – 6 PM	Drive home while listening to the radio
6 – 7 PM	Prepare dinner & eat
7 – 8 PM	Watch television
8 – 9 PM	Watch television
9 – 10 PM	Putting children to bed & preparing the following days lunch
10 – 11 PM	Discussion with spouse
11 – ONWARDS	Sleep

One hour dedicated to lunch might be excessive. If you wanted, you could always dedicate some of this time towards your tools through Acceleration or Multi-tasking.

Going to the gym or doing yoga is an effective Energy Amplifier and can be a great way of jump-starting your day.

Entertainment can be a healthy complement to good living. However, it can be excessive when you find yourself consuming hours of your time watching television or movies at the expense of honoring commitments to yourself. If you prefer, you can spend this time using your new tools.

Listening to the radio while driving is a great example of Multi-tasking. However, if you want to use the time in the car more constructively, why not reinforce the ULS through Mind Scripting. This is a tool that works well accompanying such routine tasks. For example, you could also Mind Script while walking around the mall, shopping or cooking.

TRACKING YOUR COMMITMENTS

It is difficult to manage what you do not measure. Would it make sense to manage a business without tracking its expenses? Of course not, and that is why any good business keeps an accurate record of its finances. Likewise, if you want to manage your commitment to the ULS, you will benefit from measuring that commitment on a regular basis. By tracking your commitments you gather valuable information that will provide insights on how to improve your performance in the future. That is why you are advised to use a weekly Commitment Tracker. The Commitment Tracker will help solidify the choices you have made and allow you to apply the tools more effectively. It must be stressed that the tracker is designed to help you improve your application of the tools and should not to be used as a measure of your self-worth. This is particularly important to keep in mind especially for those who have a Productivity addiction.

The following steps will illustrate how to use the Commitment Tracker:

i) Determine weekly commitment

The Commitment Tracker allows you to decide how often you wish to commit to each of the tools on a weekly basis. For example, if you decide that you want to work on the tools once a day, for five days a week, simply write down "5" in the Desired Weekly Frequency column.

ii) Track your weekly performance

Once you have established your desired weekly commitments, simply use the Commitment Tracker to record how often you do each of the tools daily. For example, if you did the Tapping into the ULS exercise once on Friday, you would write the number '1' in the corresponding box. And if you did not do the Tapping into the ULS on Wednesday, you would write '0' in that box.

iii) Total your results

At the end of the week, total the number of times you used each of the tools.

iv) Compare results with the Desired Weekly Frequency

Divide your results for each tool with your goal for the week and multiply by 100%. These calculations measure your commitment to each tool on a percentage basis (Weekly Percentage).

v) Calculate the Weekly Commitment Result

Add up the weekly percentages calculated in (iv) and divide by the number of tools you are working on. This number will give you your overall weekly commitment to the program on a percentage basis (Weekly Commitment Result).

Do your best to avoid the tendency of measuring your worthiness of love and acceptance on the results. Remember you are worthy of love as you are regardless of whether you achieve 5% or a 100% of your commitments. The purpose of this tool is to peacefully explore opportunities to better enhance the commitments you make to yourself.

Measuring your performance using the Commitment Tracker will help you assess the tools you wish to give more attention to. Where you have identified areas that need improvement, take the time to study what you can do differently. Once you are aware of a challenge, simply apply your creativity towards overcoming it. Remember, every problem has a solution, and the answers are within you.

For an example of this exercise, please refer to the next page.

Tracking Your Commitments – Example

STEP 1: Determine your Desired Weekly Frequency based on how many times a week you want to commit to each of the tools.

STEP 2: Record the number of times you do each tool everyday.

STEP 3: At the end of the week, total the number of times you did each tool.

TOOLS	DESIRED WEEKLY FRE-QUENCY	MON	TUE	WED	THUR	FRI	SAT	SUN	ACHIEVED WEEKLY FREQUENCY	WEEKLY PERCENTAGE (WP)
Awareness Journal	5	1	1	1	0	0	1	0	4	80%
Tapping into the ULS	5	1	0	0	0	1	0	0	2	40%
Mind Scripting	5	1	1	1	0	1	0	0	4	80%
Lucid Living	5	0	1	1	0	0	0	0	2	40%
Unconditional Love Rewards Program	5	0	1	0	1	0	1	0	3	60%

STEP 4: Calculate the Weekly Percentage (WP) for each tool by dividing the Achieved Weekly Frequency with the Desired Weekly Frequency (eg. 3/5=0.6). Multiply this number by 100% to give you a percentage (0.6 X 100%=60%).

STEP 5: Calculate your Weekly Commitment Result by adding all your WPs and dividing by the total number of tools (eg. 80% + 40% + 80% + 40% + 60% = 300%. 300% divided by 5= 60%)

WEEKLY COMMITMENT RESULT

60%

SELF-COACHING

While committing to the ULS, wouldn't it be nice to have someone by your side who you could turn to for guidance and inspiration? The good news is that you do have someone, and that someone is you. Your ability to keep commitments to yourself will heavily depend on the support you give yourself. The final tool for the Keeping the Commitment section is self-coaching. Learning to self-coach requires learning to be there for yourself. To play the role of a self-coach, you can have fun by assuming an alternate personality that has all the qualities you would expect from a coach. You could even use someone you know. This personality could have a unique way of talking and behaving in your mind that is completely different from your own. Whether you use yourself or create an alternate personality, call on your self-coach any time you want guidance.

To be an effective self-coach, you must be able to step outside of yourself and look at your situation from the perspective of a wise and caring friend. As an introduction to self-coaching, this book will now briefly touch on the following four critical aspects of self-coaching: i) Passion for Self-Development, ii) Effective Communication, iii) Pep Talk, and iv) Self-Reflection.

Passion for Self-Development

Your most important role as a self-coach is to facilitate the experience of the ULS in a spirit of exploration and fun. By nurturing your enthusiasm for this process, you will automatically realize the energy to honor your commitments to yourself.

Effective Communication

One of the most important attributes of a good coach is the ability to communicate. In order for you to willingly accept recommendations from your self-coach, your self-coach needs to create an environment conducive to open communication. Learning how to listen is crucial to creating such an environment. Only when a coach listens can he or she provide proper advice or encouragement.

Unfortunately, the art of listening to ourselves without judgment is not a skill that we are taught. What stops many people from listening to themselves effectively is that they are afraid of what they will discover. Our addictions can make us feel that certain emotions or thoughts are unacceptable. This may cause us to avoid our feelings and make the common mistake of rushing to find solutions without fully understanding what is going on. The Awareness Journal is an excellent tool to facilitate this listening process. It uses a compassionate approach to attaining a deepened understanding of your emotional state.

How your self-coach structures his advice will also determine how readily you will accept and act on it. Whenever your self-coach wants to provide constructive criticism, he or she should look to implement the sandwich approach, where the criticism conveyed is cushioned inside two positive comments. By acknowledging the positive, your self-coach disarms your potential resistance and helps you openly consider a new way of looking at things.

Pep Talk

When a team is losing its motivation, the pep talk is one of the most useful tools at a coach's disposal. Watching some coaches adeptly charge their teams with positive emotion can be inspirational. On the other hand, watching coaches who stunt their athletes' performance by yelling or criticizing them can be heart wrenching. Your self-coach is constantly talking to you, and whether that talk serves to inspire or discourage plays a significant role in how you meet life's challenges.

Imagine how you would feel if someone was putting you down all day long? Some of us talk to ourselves in this manner. Just as this type of coaching can inhibit an athlete, it can be equally destructive in your personal life.

If you want to use your self-coach effectively, you will benefit by learning the art of pep talking. When you need to boost your motivation, you can use a pep talk to reinforce why you are working on the tools of the ULS and how it is benefiting you.

When you speak to yourself with the intent of uplifting your mind, try charging your words with emotions like love, faith and courage. By doing this, you endow your words with a greater power to influence you. For some tips on pep talking, study Muhammad Ali. He was a master of self-talk. His ability to use the power of words to transform his psyche is inspirational. Even when the entire world doubted his capabilities, you could hear him saying "I am the greatest," and soon the whole world agreed with him.

Self-Reflection

In order to make meaningful recommendations for improvement, your self-coach must evaluate how you are doing by assessing trends and key issues. The intent of this self-reflection is not to judge yourself, but to work towards making the tools more effective in helping you reclaim your freedom. That is why it is recommended that your self-coach fill out a Self-Reflection form on a monthly basis. This process will be your self-coach's chance to assess how you are doing with the tools, make recommendations for improvement and decide which areas you should focus on next.

For an example of this exercise, please refer to the next page.

Self-Reflection – Example

TOOLS	COMMENTS & RECOMMENDATIONS FOR IMPROVEMENT
Awareness Journal	I have been good at identifying my addictive behaviors throughout the day. However, I have had more difficulty breaking down the components of my addictions.
Tapping into the ULS	Though I have not been doing this tool every day, I think it is a great way of reminding myself how much love I can experience when I give myself permission.
Mind Scripting	I struggle with this tool because I find that the repetition of the scripts are becoming monotonous.
Lucid Living	I try to do this exercise right before going to work in the morning. The pressure of getting to work on time forces me to rush this exercise, and this prevents me from getting as much out of this tool as I probably could.
Unconditional Love Rewards Program	At first, it felt strange to reward myself for no reason, but now it is something I look forward to.

<u>Goals for Next Month:</u>

To ensure that the Mind Scripting does not remain mechanical, I will stop reading from my written script and be more spontaneous with my words.

To prevent myself from rushing through the Lucid Living, I will do this exercise right before I sleep each night.

My primary focus last month was working to break free from my Acceptance of Others addiction. I will spend more time on this addiction because it is still something I need to work on. Specifically, I will make the effort to risk any embarrassment that might arise from saying what I believe in.

THE ELUSIVE ADDICTION

The snow goose need not bathe to make itself white.
Neither need you do anything but be yourself.

LAO TZU

You have come a long way. Now that you are aware of your addictions, the ULS, and all the tools of the previous sections, it is time to examine one final addiction. Pay close attention to what you are about to read. By understanding this addiction in its entirety, you will better understand what the ULS is really about.

After becoming aware that the love and freedom you long for can be found in the ULS, it can be natural for you to want to eliminate all your addictions immediately. However, this desire can be self-destructive when you measure your worthiness of love on the outcome. This is one of the most common traps that people fall into while attempting to incorporate the ULS into their lives, and it is an addiction of its own. It is called the Elusive Addiction.

To help clarify this addiction for you, we have mapped out an example below:

Central Conditional Love Belief (CCLB):	→	Conditional Love Response (CLR):	→	Conditional Love Need (CLN):	→	Conditional Love Action (CLA):
I am not worthy of love and acceptance as I am.		I believe that I am more worthy of love and acceptance when I am in the ULS.		I need to be in the ULS all the time.		I will always give other people unconditional love.
				I need to use the tools regularly.		I will do the tools every day.
				I need to always feel love for myself.		I will force myself to feel worthy of love.

Although we stress the importance of integrating the ULS into your life, if you base your worth on how well you accept yourself it defeats the entire purpose. This tendency only creates another form of conditional love. If you are feeling bad because you have "failed" to experience the ULS, you likely have the Elusive Addiction. This addiction is called *elusive* because the very tools that help liberate you from existing chains end up creating a new one. This addiction is so subtle that it eludes many people. However, it can be easily avoided by understanding some key points about the ULS.

Firstly, you do not need to progress in order to reap the benefits of the ULS. That is the beauty of the CULB, "I am worthy of love and acceptance as I am." No amount of success or progress towards integrating the ULS will make you any more worthy of love than you already are. The fundamental purpose of the ULS is to feel unconditional love for yourself independent of your progress. This transformation can be experienced right now. You can choose to feel worthy of love and acceptance in every moment.

Here is an example of how you can reverse the Elusive Addiction using the same process you have used for other addictions:

Central Unconditional Love Belief (CULB):	Unconditional Love Response (ULR):	Unconditional Love Choice (ULC):	Unconditional Love Action (ULA):
I am worthy of love and acceptance as I am.	I am worthy of love and acceptance regardless of whether I feel worthy of love and acceptance all the time.	I choose to make the ULS a prominent part of my life because of the freedom and joy it can bring.	I will try my best to express unconditional love to myself and others.
			I will use the tools I have learned.
			I will explore and play in this new world of possibilities.
			I will not judge my progress.

In the above example, notice that the motivation behind experiencing the ULS comes from the freedom of choice, as opposed to the fear of not proving your self-worth that is characteristic of the CLS.

The Elusive Addiction is such a prevalent addiction that some of the students in the past have chosen to address it in their Mind Scripting and Lucid Living exercises. For example, in your Mind Script you might include a statement such as "I am worthy of love regardless of whether I feel it all the time. I will not judge my progress in the ULS because nothing can make me more worthy of love than I am right now." While Lucid Living some people imagine themselves feeling good, even when they are caught up in an addiction.

This brings up another important point about the Elusive Addiction. You are not encouraged to force change on yourself. The ULS is not dependent on being perfect or controlling your feelings. Although experiencing unconditional love may make you feel great, the ULS is not about always feeling great either. Instead, it is about being aware of yourself and letting yourself be who you are. If you feel frustrated in life, let yourself be frustrated. If you feel afraid or sad, let yourself feel these emotions. There is no longer anything to be, or anything to prove in the ULS.

No matter how much you break free from your addictions, the ultimate freedom of the ULS is to accept yourself as you are. That means you are worthy of love even if you have addictions. If you can understand this, then the journey that you have taken was a journey to end all journeys – a journey that ends the need to become anything at all and gives you the freedom to be who you are.

10

As Brandon turned the last page, he felt the burden of years of conditioning being lifted from his shoulders. He looked around him at the majestic Himalayas and felt the world opening up. Brandon realized that everything he sought through climbing was available to him right at that moment. In the distance he saw the peak of the mighty Everest and smiled. He wondered how different the climb would be now that he knew the truth. He was Born on the Mountaintop.

NEW BEGINNINGS – A NOTE OF FAREWELL

Dear Reader,

You are Born on the Mountaintop.

Now that you know this truth, there is nowhere left to climb and nothing more to prove. The love and acceptance you have been searching for is right here, where you are. If you choose, nothing can stop you from realizing the freedom to live the way you want. Nothing can stop you from experiencing the joy of unleashing your spirit and the peace of mind that is your birthright. The choice is yours.

You are now a pioneer of unconditional love. How the ULS will unfold in your life and the world is yours to discover. As you forge your path of freedom and begin to challenge the notions of what you need to be in this world, there may be times when you face some resistance. Whatever you do, try not to lose heart. Your freedom is connected to the freedom of all life on this planet. Since many people have yet to realize they are worthy of love as they are, they are destroying themselves and the earth out of sheer desperation to fulfill their addictions.

Fortunately, one person makes a difference. By continuing to commit to unconditional love, you help give birth to a new consciousness where we can stop chasing after what we do not need and start loving ourselves for who we really are. Such a love has the power to help us put aside our differences and work together to build a world centered not around fear but around love. This love transcends space and time. When you immerse yourself in it, all the souls who have lived for love and cried for freedom walk with you. Then, in your every step, you help create the path that frees the world.

Satyam and Freedom Malhotra

ABOUT THE AUTHORS

Satyam and Freedom Malhotra are co-founders of *Me Magic*, an organization dedicated to empowering people to break free from the chains of their minds and hearts. Combining their experience in health care and business, they empower people with practical ways to free their minds on a personal and professional level.

FREEDOM MALHOTRA

Throughout his life, Freedom has seen his share of ups and downs. He began his career as a struggling entrepreneur to eventually becoming a corporate executive spearheading multi-million dollar deals. His educational background includes an MBA from the University of Western Ontario. Freedom consults with organizations committed to reinventing the workplace. He helps companies unleash the passion, teamwork and creativity of their employees through the revolutionary business applications of Born on the Mountaintop.

"You cannot become who you want until you confront who you are." Freedom Malhotra has always strived to live his life true to these words. From a young age, he dedicated himself to the pursuit of personal freedom and finding out why most of us never experience the love and acceptance we seek. Refusing to accept the dissatisfaction, and conflict of everyday life, he sought to understand the root cause of these problems. This quest led him to realize many of the insights of Born on the Mountaintop. When the answers he sought began to surface, he was amazed by how simple and revolutionary they were and how much they could positively transform the lives of others.

SATYAM MALHOTRA

As a Physical Therapist, Satyam Malhotra has always endeavored to understand the psychological forces that create the stress and anxiety underlying many physical ailments. In his search for answers, Satyam practiced alternative forms of healing while traveling through India. Sitting across from his patients, he realized that there is something fundamentally unhealthy about people's perception that leads to the disharmony they experience. It became clear to him that, regardless of what form of treatment people receive, they will continue to experience needless stress and illness unless they challenge the way they have been conditioned to think.

His desire to address health problems on this deeper level has culminated in the breakthroughs he shares in the Born on the Mountaintop experience. Satyam provides tools that help people realize a complete acceptance of themselves and their surroundings. And this is one of the keys to living a free and healthy life.

HOW TO CONTACT THE AUTHORS

If Born on the Mountaintop has made a positive difference in your life, Satyam and Freedom would love to hear about your experiences. Also, if you have any information you think will help their ongoing research into better ways of reclaiming people's lives and unleashing their spirits, feel free to contact them. Simply email: *connect@memagic.com*

BORN ON THE MOUNTAINTOP

Could someone you know benefit from reading Born on the Mountaintop? It's the perfect present for anyone. It's insightful, revolutionary and opens the door to a world of exploration. Most importantly, you will be giving someone one of the greatest gifts possible – the gift of freedom.

To purchase your copies visit a local bookstore, order online at **www.memagic.com** or send us this order form to the address below. Special discounts are available for bulk purchases. For details, please write to us at the address below or email us at **order@memagic.com**.

ORDER FORM

Please send me _____ copies of Born on the Mountaintop at $32.95 CDN or $33.65 USD each (including shipping). I have enclosed a cheque made payable to *Me Magic* in the amount of $ _____ CDN or USD (please circle one). Orders outside of Canada and the USA please visit **www.memagic.com**.

Full Name:_____

Address:_____

_____

City:_____ State/Province:_____

Postal/Zip Code:_____ Telephone:_____

Email Address:_____

ME MAGIC
P.O. Box 81053
47B Harbour Square
Toronto, ON
M5J 2R0
Canada

Please allow four to six weeks for delivery.

BORN ON THE MOUNTAINTOP
THE WEEKEND EXPERIENCE

Challenging our social conditioning is not easy, especially when we live in a world that continues to reinforce our psychological addictions. That is why Satyam and Freedom Malhotra have developed the Born on the Mountaintop weekend experience. This course is an opportunity to break away from your daily routine and invest the time required to realize what being Born on the Mountaintop means to you.

Freedom and Satyam are dynamic facilitators who create a fun and interactive learning environment where you will be free to share your views and learn from others. Their compassionate approach creates a non-threatening atmosphere that allows you to explore your inner world. There will also be opportunities for one-on-one coaching to answer questions and help apply insights specifically to your life.

Join the authors of Born on the Mountaintop for a weekend that you will never forget. For more information visit **www.memagic.com**.

BORN ON THE MOUNTAINTOP
REINVENTING THE WORKPLACE

Through their dynamic speeches, seminars and workshops, Freedom and Satyam can help revolutionize the culture of your organization through unleashing the passion, teamwork and creativity of your employees.

If you would like to learn more about bringing the Born on the Mountaintop experience to your organization, contact *Me Magic* at: **connect@memagic.com**.